T0102400

Spiritual Nutrition

Other Books by Mike Radice

Professional Money Raising for Schools, 2014
ISBN-10: 1500372706
ISBN-13: 978-15003727705

Conscious Nutrition, 2021
ISBN: 9781393387688

Spiritual Nutrition

Mike Radice

BOOKS

Winchester, UK
Washington, USA

JOHN HUNT PUBLISHING

First published by O-Books, 2024
O-Books is an imprint of John Hunt Publishing Ltd., 3 East St., Alresford,
Hampshire SO24 9EE, UK
office@jhpbooks.com
www.johnhuntpublishing.com
www.o-books.com

For distributor details and how to order please visit the 'Ordering' section on our website.

Text copyright: Mike Radice 2023

ISBN: 978 1 80341 384 6
978 1 80341 385 3 (ebook)
Library of Congress Control Number: 2022951110

All rights reserved. Except for brief quotations in critical articles or reviews, no part of this book may be reproduced in any manner without prior written permission from the publishers.

The rights of Mike Radice as author have been asserted in accordance with the Copyright, Designs and Patents Act 1988.

A CIP catalogue record for this book is available from the British Library.

Design: Lapiz Digital Services

UK: Printed and bound by CPI Group (UK) Ltd, Croydon, CR0 4YY
Printed in North America by CPI GPS partners

The author of this book does not dispense medical advice or prescribe the use of any technique as a form of treatment for physical, emotional, or medical problems without the advice of a physician, either directly or indirectly. The intent of the author is only to offer information of a general nature to help you in your quest for emotional and spiritual well-being. In the event you use any of the information in this book for yourself, which is your constitutional right, the author and the publisher assume no responsibility for your actions.

We operate a distinctive and ethical publishing philosophy in all areas of our business, from our global network of authors to production and worldwide distribution.

Contents

Acknowledgements

I want to thank everyone who helped bring this project to completion. Unfortunately, there are too many to list here, so I'll choose those who provided the most substantive help. I'll present the helpers in alphabetical order except for my friend, Mick Landaiche, the brave soul who read the entire manuscript early when it was horrible. Mick is a psychotherapist in Pittsburgh, so he's wired and trained for kindness.

Here are the rest of the helpers. Many bows to each of them.

Zel and Reuben Allen of Vegetarians in Paradise from whom I took several vegan cooking classes. They started the engine on the topic for me.

Chef AJ, who introduced me to cooking without salt, oil and sugar. Until then, I had no idea it was even a thing.

Dr. Gabriel Cousens who introduced me to the concept of spiritual nutrition.

David Ghiyam, my Teacher at The Kabbalah Centre who helped me rethink the meaning of kosher.

Dale Jaffey at Mind Matters Restorative Hypnotherapy who introduced me to Chef AJ.

Dr. David Meinke, The University of Toledo professor who offered the Psychology of Conscious doctoral-level class opening my window to the spiritual world of energy. The course also dislodged me from religion and dropped me into the world of the cosmos.

Peter May for showing me that plants talk.

Magenta Pixie for introducing me to the Lemurian diet in her book Lessons from a Living Lemuria.

Cantor Juval Porat of Beth Chayim Chadashim for analyzing the Torah in a way that helped me see its plant-based intent.

Tom Ryu of Shumei America who taught me about Natural Agriculture and its link to a healthy body and spirit.

Philipp Schardt who led me from Light Activation to Brotherhood of Light membership at the Modern Mystery School.

Courtney Shelburne, Plant Medicine Healer who introduced me to plant spirits and how they heal us.

Steven Todd Smith, one of my Reiki Master Teachers, for leading me through the process of becoming a Master Teacher.

Much gratitude to the following public libraries, their reference librarians and their brave employees at the checkout desk: Cleveland, Glendale, Hartford, Los Angeles City and County, New York, Pasadena, Santa Monica and Toledo.

The following academic libraries that granted access to their collections: California Polytechnic State University, Northeastern University, University of California at Los Angeles and The University of Toledo.

The TrueNorth Health Center for showing me the connection between clean eating and physical health.

Anthony William whose books taught me about plant messaging.

The following coffee shops that gave me work space in exchange for coffee: Javista Organic Coffee Bar, Boys Town Starbucks, Liberation Coffee House, Coffee Connection, Philz Coffee and Rosebud Coffee.

Much thanks to Miami University (OH), where I earned my bachelor's degree. Without Miami's guidance, education and encouragement, this book would have never materialized.

I want to thank my parents, Louis and Joann Radice, who supported my education and growth throughout my childhood. I also want to thank my maternal grandmother, Elizabeth Ann Vetter. Grandma was a nurse who had the patience to teach me how to read when my eye muscles weren't working correctly. Without her help, I would have never gone to college and you wouldn't be reading this book.

Introduction

What Is This Book About?

Spiritual Nutrition charts a path enabling you to be an integral part of the New Earth. The Earth is returning to a higher, less dense vibrational energy. It's nearing the end of a cycle of cleansing the old and bringing in the new. You don't want to be left behind, which is why you're reading this page. The New Earth is a worldwide transition to a higher vibrational energy. Energy is the vitalizing property of matter; the active, attractive, generative, gravitative and positive principle of creation. It is also the basis of the atom and the stuff that turns on the light bulb, makes us warm and boots the computer. On a spiritual level, the force, or life principle, makes Mind.

Mind is the thing humans use to think and communicate.

You can see the transition in the changes you're experiencing on the planet such as global warming, COVID, fires, political upheaval, etc. The Mayans ended their calendar in 2012. But the calendar's conclusion wasn't about the world's end. It was about the end of the old era and the beginning of the final transition to the New Earth.

The Mayans weren't alone in their prediction. Christians today call it Armageddon. Hindus call it Vishna's return on the White Horse. Muslims call it The Hour. Jews call it the rebuilding of the Third Temple. Tibetan and Indian Buddhists call it the return of Shambhala. (The term "India" refers to the country.)

To illustrate this from a Christian perspective, I'll borrow wording posited by the Seventh-day Adventist's website and compare it to the New Earth perspective. The two are the same except for the language. The Adventists are Christians who, in my opinion, have the clearest wording of what the *Bible* says about the transition. Every religion has a story, but this sect of

Christianity comes the closest to the New Earth's explanation. Christianity is the primary religious understanding of much of the Western world so it's important to understand its position.

According to the Adventists, Jesus will be returning at what most Christians call a Second Coming. Christians believe that Jesus, born about 2020 years ago, was the Messiah (Christ), the Son of God who was crucified for the sins of humanity before rising from the dead. The Adventists believe that people still alive on the planet will be joined by those who were raised from the dead and everyone will be taken to Heaven with Him.

The Adventists also believe that Heaven is not the final destination. According to them, the *Bible* reports they will stay in heaven with Jesus for 1,000 years (a Millennium) while the rest of humanity goes through a judgment. This judgment also impacts Satan, his followers and his angels who will be destroyed once and for all. The earth will be burned completely with a purifying fire.

From a New Earth perspective, which is the perspective of this book and the Lightworkers, the Adventist beliefs transfer as follows:

- The word "Heaven" is another word for the New Earth.
- The "believers who are still alive" and "those who were raised from the dead" are those who are aware of the transition and whose vibration has raised enough to "ascend" and be a natural part of the transition.
- A "nonbeliever" is someone whose vibration is low and has more karma to work out before joining the others.
- Jesus' Second Coming is the return of Christ Consciousness and not the return of the man Jesus.

Please note that there is no primary source or archaeological evidence that Jesus the man existed. We learned about him from others reporting on his life and work 100 years after the man

4

died. Those reports are secondary sources, so we cannot rely on them. There is scant evidence of several men similar to him, and perhaps the New Testament Jesus is either one of them or a composite under the "Christ Consciousness" umbrella.

What is Christ Consciousness? It is a universal truth, someone's last name. Christ consciousness is the spiritual essence hidden at the core of each individual, at the nucleus of every atom of creation. It is the infinite Intelligence present in all creation. Christ means "anointed of God" or "chosen by God". It is the English term for the Greek word Khristós, which is the translation of the Hebrew word, Messiah. Followers of Jesus believed him to be the Messiah as prophesied in the *Torah*. Therefore, they often wrote Jesus Christ, meaning Jesus is the Khristós or Messiah. Buddha was Buddha Christ. Gandhi was Gandhi Christ. Lightworkers are Lightworker Christ. Most of us have at least a kernel of it, albeit it could be buried and looking for a way out.

The New Earth is the final destination predicted by the Adventists and there are parallels in the descriptions.

- Yes, the old Earth will transform through a cleansing process into a higher vibrational state, and we are in that process currently.
- The cleansing will be more difficult and perhaps impossible for lower vibrational individuals (the judged and Satan's army and angels).
- The planet's cleansing is that horrific end the Bible predicts; the fires, floods, earthquakes, etc. are cleansing tools.

Regardless what religions call it or how they represent it, they all know "something" is coming. Just what that something is depends on many factors, which I'll discuss in this book. It's impossible to predict what's going to happen in the future given that everyone's sheer existence changes the situation every second of the day. Regardless, most spiritual teachers—and religions—predict opposition to the change. Ultimately, there will be pure beauty and delight with a considerably higher energy vibration. The higher the vibration, the more communal and peaceful the environment.

Before they became religions, the original purpose of the spiritual practices was to prepare us for the transition back to the "New Earth". That's why a God—whatever the God was that showed up and said it—appeared to the Jews and invited them on the journey. We're told it's why Jesus was born and taught love. We're told it's why Allah created the world in six days and sent Abraham, Moses, David and Muhammad to reject idolatry and polytheism. It's why Zen and Tibetan Buddhists emphasize the oneness coming from meditation.

I am not a doomsayer, although I might sound like one. Automatic or forced transitions have a pain element. But the pain is a good thing because it teaches us something and helps clear the path. We throw off the old during any transition and bring in the new (or let it roll in). Sometimes the "throwing off" is forced; other times, we choose it because we know it's good for us. I've been through forced and chosen transitions over the years. I'm in the middle of one right now, and let me tell you, it's been weird—the weirdest of them all. If I'd encountered these events 20 years ago, I'd be in a psych ward or a jail right now. Some of these things have included a COVID-induced job loss, being hit by a car while cycling, downsizing to fit into a smaller apartment, living through my first traffic accident on the freeway and more. I know what it's all about, and I appreciate what it teaches me and how the experiences move me along. I'm grateful for it all. It's speeding and lightening my vibration every day. This is also a transition to help me serve others more completely. I've long understood my fundamental role in lifting the Earth's vibration, and that's why I wrote this book.

I am hoping that by the time you finish this book, not only will you see your transition, but you'll want to speed it along and smooth the way. Many people see rough times and events as permanent disasters with lifelong adverse effects that they can't shake. The events become a part of their life stories: "My husband divorced me, that &#%!@. I have Attention Deficit Disorder, so I can't hold a job. My father beat me as a child, so I am permanently depressed." I have tremendous empathy for everyone who experienced these struggles. I know the experiences were painful, and I'm sorry that they happened. I hope you will consider them in a new light as painful teaching tools versus the end of the road. You will heal from them, forgive people and use what you've learned to build the kind of life you want while lifting others. The transition could be a rough ride if you don't do this.

I will provide all the tools you need in this book to lift your vibrational energy and enable your smooth transition with the New Earth. Improving yourself likewise lifts everyone around you.

This Introduction chapter fills you in on what's happening in the world and how the book can help.

Chapter One rethinks the definition of food to include what we put into our mouths and take into our spirit. The balance of the book discusses how to find the best kinds of each and how to use them to lift yourself. This chapter also discusses the spiritual nature of plants. This book promotes a vegan diet as the best for ascension, so you'll need to know some things about the plants.

Chapter Two summarizes what world religions say about diet to help us unpack our childhood teachings.

Chapter Three talks about food quality and vibration. The highest quality plant foods have the highest vibration, which transfers to you when you eat them.

Chapters Four and Five talk about coagulators and anticoagulators. Coagulators block fluid and energy flow in your body. Anticoagulators enable the flow. You want maximum flow within to raise your vibration and be physically healthy.

Chapter Six helps you identify food needs based on what your body wants. Everyone's body is different.

Chapter Seven provides steps and tools to transition to a higher vibrational diet.

Chapter Eight discusses progressing to an entirely vegan diet, and advice on what changes to expect and tips on how to deal with them.

The Resources section provides tools for further learning.

Before we begin, I'd like to stop and define a few terms I frequently use.

Terms

This section defines some of the most frequently-used terms that have multiple meanings in the conventional and spiritual worlds. Some terms include vegan versus plant-based, religious versus spiritual, dimensions and karma. Without these clarifications, you may get confused. To date, you may have picked up your understandings from pop culture, religious teaching or a mathematical understanding, but I will set those aside and regroup you. Other new terms will occasionally appear throughout the book, but I'll define them as I go along.

Conventional Vegan versus Spiritual Nutrition Vegan versus Plant-based: You will find that I sometimes use the term "vegan" to describe a spiritual nutritional path. As with any term, definitions evolve with people choosing sides and finding new ways to fight over definitions. The Vegan Society swears that their definition has been the correct one since the beginning of time, and perhaps that is true; it is the most quoted on social media. But when I became a vegan over 30 years ago, I operated under a different definition that I understood was the true definition: the exclusive eating of plants. I believe that most nonvegans see it that way as well.

It's impossible to know what's true. The definitions are human-made, and there is no "Definition God" declaring a truth. For now, we can agree to disagree. But I use the term "vegan" in this book to describe the recommended foods to consume, and my definition is not theirs.

I'll outline their definition and mine below. When I use the term "vegan" in this book, I mean Spiritual Nutrition Vegan, not Conventional Vegan. I present this as a disclaimer for the balance of the book.

Conventional Vegan: According to the Vegan Society, veganism is "a philosophy and way of living which seeks to exclude—as far as is possible and practicable—all forms of exploitation of and cruelty to animals."

As you can see, diet isn't mentioned. Plant-eating is an outcome of the philosophy.

Spiritual Nutrition Vegan: Here, I present the definition used in this book. For brevity, I will lop off the words "Spiritual Nutrition" and leave the word "Vegan" to stand alone. My definition is, "A spiritual practice of eating foods with the highest spiritual vibration, which includes fruits, vegetables, grains and honey."

You will also hear the term "plant-based" used to describe plant-eaters. The term was introduced when groups of vegans turned angry and violent toward nonvegans for not following their understanding of vegan practices. The phrase "Plant-based" was coined by the nonviolent to distance themselves from the hate. Plant-based eaters eat only plants but may do it primarily for health or environmental reasons. It may or may not be about the animals.

Religion versus Spiritual versus Spirituality: I often use the terms religion, spiritual and Spirit throughout the book. They aren't interchangeable, and I will explain them here for clarity.

According to the *Merriam-Webster Dictionary*, religion is the belief in a god or a group of gods; something people turn to for comfort in a time of crisis; an organized system of beliefs, ceremonies and rules used to worship a god or a group of gods.

Spiritual, according to *Merriam-Webster*, is relating to, consisting of, or affecting Spirit.

Spiritual means different things to different people. In addition to the dictionary's definition, there are many others that I commonly see. I list them here and will let you know the ones I think fit the book's storyline.

1. It means religion, being religious and following the laws and traditions of religion.
2. It means believing in a central god Source.
3. It has to do with the soul and the Spirit.
4. It's associated with the New Age Movement, psychics, astrology and the paranormal.
5. It's anything nonphysical.
6. It means meditation, yoga, the expansion of consciousness and spiritual awakening.
7. It's something beyond comprehension.

Here is the definition I will use in this book. It's the one I most commonly see in the Lightworker community, and it makes the most sense from my experience. "The universal life energy empowering all beings, thoughts and transitions to develop spiritual awakening." That definition is a combination of two, three and six above.

I use "Spirit" to represent spirituality when referring to the energetic entity or entities that help influence us. Spirit takes the universal life energy and organizes it to help us lift our vibration and become one within the Fifth Dimension. I'll define the Fifth Dimension in a later section. For now, it's the higher vibrational state representing the New Earth.

Dimensions: A dimension is an energy vibration. But what is energy? Here is a standard dictionary definition: "The capacity for doing work. Energy may exist in potential, kinetic, thermal, electrical, chemical, nuclear or other forms." If you could talk to Albert Einstein, he'd tell you that energy is the everything of everything, which is the same meaning used by energy healers. Left-brained science and right-brained energy healers agree. Are you still lost? Let me try this another way.

I'm an energy healer (also called a "Lightworker"). I access energy and channel it to others for healing, but I'm a graduate-degreed scientist of psychology and history. I live and operate in both worlds and neither contradicts the other. I will, however, dig deeper from the Lightworker's point of view because the book sees things from this angle, but I will also attempt to merge the meanings from the two positions and simplify them in digestible language. Here goes: Energy is the invisible stuff that makes up everything we encounter through our senses and intuition. The invisible elements include the unmeasurable unknown and the measurable known, such as atoms, quarks and waves. Energy turns on the lights and warms our bodies from within, but the magnetic pull also brings the cosmos together, assembling the dust and giving everything life and purpose. Spirit is pure energy. Energy is spiritual.

Energy is also a vibration, which we learned in high school. Remember Einstein's formula $E=mc^2$? "Energy equals mass times the speed of light squared." The equation means that energy and mass (matter) are interchangeable; they are simply different forms of the same thing. When energy is slowed, it binds together to form mass, so mass is energy at a lower vibration. This means that the faster an energy's vibration, the lighter it is and the more challenging it is to see or measure. Spirit operates at a very high vibration, which is why you can't see it. The high-pitched sounds only a dog can hear are at a lower vibration than Spirit, yet too high of a vibration for humans to hear. A light stream's vibrational energy is higher than an apple's energy. You can measure both but can't capture or cut up the light. A candle has a higher vibration than structural steel, which is why it's used to light a room but not to build a skyscraper.

Now, onto the meaning of an energy-based dimension. Each dimension has its left-brain mathematical and spiritual energy characteristics. The mathematical portion focuses on what can be measured. The spiritual energy portion includes life force content dyed into the energy. The higher the vibration, the more life force content. For example, a rock has less life force content than a bird. Higher vibrational energies bring happiness and inclusion. Lower vibrational energies bring binarism and anger.

Vibrational speeds are described in dimensions with stage characteristics. Left-brained scientists can describe the first four dimensions and believe there are at least one or two more. Many Lightworkers posit at least 12 dimensions but can only describe the first five or six. Just because we can't describe something doesn't mean it doesn't exist. Eventually, we will see more of the unknown and be able to describe it. We once thought the world was flat until we figured out it was round. We once thought the Sun revolved around the Earth until we learned otherwise.

The First Dimension has the lowest vibration, and the Twelfth Dimension has the highest. Scientists are aware of the Fifth, but they struggle to define it. Lightworkers have definitions through the Fifth in part because so many of us experience the Fifth. There are probably more dimensions than 12 because how would we know there wasn't? We can only describe what exists a step or two behind where we are. Most people are Third Dimensional, and Lightworkers are Fourth Dimensional with Fifth Dimensional access.

I'll summarize the dimensions one through five because that is as far as the book takes you. When we say "levels", the reality is that they are not as mutually exclusive as they sound. Each higher level incorporates the characteristics of the prior level much like Jean Piaget's Stages of Cognitive Development or Lawrence Kohlberg's for Moral Development. As someone progresses from one level to the next, the lower-level features fade away but do not necessarily vanish. You can think of it as a bleed along each dimensional edge.

The First Dimension (1D) is the most basic. It's commonly defined as any line connecting two points without width or depth—only length in its purest form. There are no sentient beings in this dimension since sentient beings have form. So, there is nothing there to have a sense of self, others or the broader Universe. When I say "sentient", I mean the capacity to experience feelings and sensations, a being with consciousness. Puppies have consciousness; rocks do not. When I say Universe, I mean the presence of all things, including what we can experience and not experience.

The Second Dimension (2D) has length and width. Sentient beings exist in this dimension, including insects and most animals. However, their vibrations are too low to have a sense of self or others and certainly not of the broader Universe.

The Third Dimension (3D) has length, breadth and depth. Sentient beings exist in this dimension and that includes most humans. In 3D, humans have a sense of self, but most struggle with a sense of others or an understanding of the broader Universe. They can understand it intellectually, but they have trouble feeling or relating to it. It is also the dimension of dualism, binarism and a belief in the absoluteness of rules, rituals, governments, traditions and the march of time. A 3D being may feel someone else's pain, but they believe that the behaviors and conditions of others stop them from getting what they want. It's like the parent of a child who regularly misbehaves in school. Yes, they love the child. Yes, they worry about the child. And yes, they worry about themselves and their reputations. Often, their punishments and responses center on how the child's behavior affects them.

The Fourth Dimension (4D) includes length, breadth and depth. The 4D sentient beings have self-awareness and awareness of the needs of others, but they lack a sense of the broader Universe beyond what they can intellectually explain. This dimension also puts them into a space-time continuum, meaning that time is no longer linear. Sentient beings have a "service-to-others" orientation. Examples include Buddhist Monk Thich Nhat Hanh, Gandhi and St. Francis of Assisi. Jesus of Nazareth—as described—was closer to 5D.

The Fifth Dimension (5D) is a place where there's a consciousness of love, joy, peace, freedom and compassion. Spiritual wisdom prevails, and everything exists without boundaries. Beings (often in crystalline or light form) have a service-to-others orientation. They also experience frequent synchronizations and focus on the present moment. Linear time and space don't exist, and there is no illusion of separation or limitation.

Do you see yourself in one of these dimensions? Two of them? Maybe three? If you're on this page, you're likely on the continuum between mid-3D and 5D.

Karma: The idea that karma is a moral justice system in which positive thoughts bring good things and negativity is a curse is incorrect. That's a pop culture definition. Karma is simply the sum of a person's actions in this and previous states of existence, viewed as deciding their fate and lessons for future existences.

Karma is the Sanskrit word for action, and action rules our lives. The word karma is rooted in Hinduism, but the understanding is shared between Hinduism and Buddhism. The Hindu version, which I rely on more heavily than the Buddhist version, believes that the soul survives death in an energy form and is reborn into a new body, taking the inheritance of the behavior and unlearned lessons from the previous life into the latest incarnation. The inheritance becomes the lessons to learn in the next life. If those lessons are not learned, the karmic activity continues into the next life.

The soul is the entity that animates the body and gives it life.

The Buddhist version focuses more on the push-pull effect. You put something out there, and it comes back to you and affects others. This is true, of course, but I like the broader Hindu version in part because I experience it regularly.

Back to the Hindu version. Let's say, for example, that you were in a marital relationship with someone in your previous life, and it ended badly because of your poor behavior. Poor behavior is a lower vibrational activity, slowing your soul's vibration and preventing it from joining the community of one, the ultimate goal. Anger, aggression, control and negativity are lower vibrational energies. Peace, kindness, love, beauty and community are higher energy vibrations.

The bad ending of your marriage, which was your fault, created karma between you and lowered your vibration. Now, you need to raise your vibration to clear the karma and to move on. This is your soul's goal. So, you encounter that same person or situation in the next life, but now you're the victim. This enables you to experience what you did and to learn from it. If you don't learn from it, it will return in your subsequent lives until you do.

What is the "next" life in this universe with time? It isn't really "next" in a calendar sort of way. You can encounter these same spiritual beings in parallel universes and lives which are the equivalent of "next".

Transition to the New Earth

Everything operates in cycles—our bodies, our trajectories, our families, our communities and even our ideas. The cells of our body switch over every seven years. You go to school, graduate, work and maybe have a family. The family has a family and so forth. Cities change, too. I recently saw side-by-side pictures of a section of East 6th Street in Downtown Cleveland, my hometown. One photo was from 1920 and the other from 2021. By 2021, real estate developers had replaced all the buildings from the '20s. Even the physical street looked different—fewer people, fewer cars, less chaos.

Change is inevitable and automatic. You can influence it, but you can't stop it. Many try—especially the physical ageing process—but it rolls out anyway. We have some control over "how" we age. My health and spiritual practices have enabled me to be the only one in my social circle who isn't on medications and is never sick (for the last 20 years, at least). I couldn't keep my appearance from age 21, yet I appear younger than my age. The same goes for the City of Cleveland. I'm sure folks tried to stop the changes to that section of East 6th Street. Cleveland is a big city, so protests to change are reflexive. Regardless, developers replaced the three to five-story brick structures with modern-day towers.

What happens to us and our communities is just a subset of what happens to the planet Earth. The Earth, a living being, has cycles manifesting in seasons, pole shifts, weather patterns, earthquakes, ice ages and vibrational changes. Seasonal changes, weather and earthquakes are easy for humans to see. Pole shifts and ice ages are harder for the average person to see. To understand them, you have to rely on left-brain science or our intuition. Vibrational upgrades are invisible to the eye yet they are experienced and managed by Lightworkers.

According to the National Aeronautics and Space Administration (NASA), "The position of Earth's magnetic north pole was first precisely located in 1831. Since then, it has gradually drifted north-northwest by more than 600 miles (1,100 kilometers), and its forward speed has increased from about ten miles (16 kilometers) per year to about 34 miles (55 kilometers) per year." The shifts manifest themselves in changes in atmospheric, weather and vibrational patterns.

Earth also has Ice Ages, which are long periods of reduction in Earth's surface and atmosphere temperature resulting in the presence or expansion of continental and polar ice sheets and alpine glaciers. Ice Ages are cyclical: Earth's climate alternates between ice ages and greenhouse periods, during which there are no glaciers on the planet. Yes, pollution contributes to warming, but warming is also a natural cycle. However, pollution seems to be helping it along.

The Universe changes, too, and Earth is a member of the Universe. By "Universe", I mean the infinity of galaxies, planets, stars and everything in and between them. The Universe has endless cycles of expansion and cooling, each beginning with a "big bang" and ending in a "big crunch". Currently, our galaxy is moving, and since it's changing positions in the broader Universe, you can expect changes on Earth. All changes create domino effects.

Here's more evidence of the change as reported on Space.com, an award-winning science news publication. The article's author, Elizabeth Howell, quoted and summarized NASA research:

The galaxies are moving away from Earth because the fabric of space itself is expanding. While galaxies themselves are on the move—the Andromeda Galaxy and the Milky Way, for example, are on a collision course—there is an overall phenomenon of redshift happening as the Universe gets bigger.

("What are Redshift and Blueshift?", 16 March 2018)

American astronomer Edwin Hubble (for whom the Hubble Space Telescope was named) was the first to describe the redshift phenomenon and tie it to an expanding Universe. "His observations, revealed in 1929, showed that nearly all galaxies he observed are moving away. This phenomenon was observed as a redshift of a galaxy's spectrum," NASA said. "This redshift appeared to be larger for faint, presumably further, galaxies. Hence, the farther a galaxy, the faster it is receding from Earth."

Cycles are cleansings, just like you might clean out a closet, convert the garage to a family room or get a college degree to change your career. Cycles throw off the old, bring in the new, and enter something into the next cycle. But there are multiple layers to the cycle we're in now. We can experience and measure the physical changes—pole shifts, rising temperatures, galaxy movement. Still, there are also spiritual-vibrational changes that we can't detect or measure with our 3D understanding and mechanical instruments. On another layer or level, the Earth is nearing the end of a vibrational cycle anticipated by world religions, spiritual guides, Lightworkers, shamans and psychics. On this other level, we're nearing the end of the cycle because Spirit sees that enough Earth humans have vibrationally progressed to end it and begin the next. Earth will no longer be a low-vibration karmic school for humans. It will return to its original purpose as a higher vibrational resting place for evolved spiritual beings. To get there, it must finish its physical cleansing and continue to increase human vibrational frequency of the planet's humans. The higher the vibration of the humans, the easier it will be for them to transition. After all, the Earth is our mother; she doesn't want us to experience pain if she can help it. She also won't intervene and do it for us. She'll provide the tools, teach us how to use them, and let us loose from there.

The Earth's cleansing process is a means of clearing all physical and emotional pollutions, and it's time for them to go.

Each cleanout tool includes a test to lift our vibration. How do my children handle it? Will they learn from it, reach each other for support to create peace and happiness and ride with it? Or will they fight each other, fight themselves and then pray for things to "Return to normal"? Earth's cleanouts include new diseases, extreme weather patterns, earthquakes, Negative Polarity (NP) exposures, pole shifts, temperature changes, etc. Once cleansed, the cycle ends: The Earth returns to its pristine, higher vibrational state—Heaven, Shambhala, Gaia or whatever your tradition calls it.

Negative Polarities are the dark forces, the energy beings who have a pure service-to-self orientation. Some beings we can see given that they incarnated into humans on the planet. Others are beyond our comprehension, such as NPs from other dimensions and "some" extraterrestrials (most are benevolent). Among those we can see are enslavers, murderers, greedy politicians, rapists, etc.

Earth is in the final phase of the cycle, and "thank you" to the Mayans for tipping us off in 2012. It's time to celebrate. It's been millions, perhaps billions of years since the Earth was a high vibrational karmic rest stop, and it has worked its way back. What lowered its vibration so long ago? Many stories abound among the ancient writings and art, but we can thank the Sumerians for beautifully chronicling it. Their writings are the best 3D measurable source available. Of course, there are other versions, and each could be a metaphor, but the storyline is the same. You can find similar storylines in Dolores Cannon's past life regression research, the Ra material, etc. The details change between the sources, but the frame is similar.

The story goes that a group of NPs from another planet faced extinction. The Universe's vibrational frequency had risen around them to the point where their lives and livelihoods were in danger. NPs operate at a lower vibration; they can't function at those higher levels and allowing them to be the majority with them kill them. They needed to do something, and Earth was one of the Universe's karmic graduation refuges and a good place to tighten the valve. Earth was a place for higher vibrational, loving souls to live once they had worked through their karma. Its vibration served as a vibrational conductor for the greater Universe. If the NPs could lower Earth's vibration, they could save themselves.

The Earth was also rich in natural resources that the NPs didn't have on their planet. Lower vibrational planets tend to have limited resources, in general. Take the Earth's resources, then lower its vibration, too, which would subsequently lower the vibration of the universe. Taking the resources to the NPs' planet wouldn't raise its vibration because what was taken wouldn't have the Earth's vibrational support once ripped from the ground.

The NPs organize and then attack with "shock and awe", making the higher vibrational beings on Earth into slaves to help the NPs gather the resources. By making them slaves, the NPs automatically lower the Earth Beings' vibration. The NPs inbreed with them to help ensure the slavery while also giving them a more easy-to-control workforce. The NPs did this using resource control, oppression, violence and fear.

Does that story sound familiar? Perhaps you remember similar ones from your high school history classes. Europeans used the same model—an archetype by then—to take control of the Americas, Africa and India in the 15th through the early 20th centuries. Archetypes are patterns of behavior that aid and influence our mental, emotional and spiritual growth. An archetype is a type of energy with a meaning. The English, Spanish, French and Portuguese languages weren't natural to the Americas nor to any other country they invaded. Catholicism was a European religion until the Spaniards rolled into Central

America, took over, and forced it on everyone. The Europeans would burst into a vulnerable area, take over, restructure the society and maintain control through disease, slavery, and fear.

If you'd like to read more about the history of the Negative Polarities on Earth, I suggest picking up a copy of *The 12th Planet* by Zecharia Sitchin. The book is one of a series written by Sitchin in which he reports on the Sumerian writings, art, etc. Conventional historians and archaeologists have studied the materials, but they report them as myths versus historical records. To conventional historians, a "myth" is a storyline that can't be verified and seems implausible by conventional understandings. In other words, when a contradiction arises in the narrative, cognitive dissonance takes over and can only be resolved by believing that material must be myth. It's a way of dismissing it without further consideration.

I understand the conventional historian point of view, although I don't agree with it. I have a PhD in history and was trained to think that way. In graduate school, we were told to only state the obvious and label the rest as possible, impossible or mythical. However, I've since learned that just because we don't understand it or can't verify it doesn't mean we should label it untrue unless we can find proof that it's false. In this case, we can't prove it's false. We assume it's false only because we can't relate to it personally, which doesn't make something untrue. Is it a myth because it involves extraterrestrials? Is it a myth because it has a spiritual layer to it? The Sumerian writings are not the only source of the story, but they are the clearest and the easiest to access. I'm not saying that this version of events is valid, but it certainly is an archetype, which means it has happened in this form more than once and can happen again. Until we can prove that it is false, it is possible.

Way back when the Negative Polarities rolled in and took over, the Earth began fighting back. We would do the same thing if a disease or negative person moved in and took us over. We'd think, "Okay. I'll work through this and then resurrect myself." That's what Earth is doing, and it's almost finished with the resurrection. About 4,500 years ago, it had put enough energy in to make difference. As partial evidence, we see the beginning of the birth of spiritual practices and religions, many extant through today. Since World War II, the Earth's transition has picked up speed with help from the Universe, and I discuss that in subsequent chapters. I think that once you read this material, you'll feel better about what's going on. I trace the final steps, discuss the role of the three waves of volunteers, present my transitional match and define "dimensions" of which the Fifth Dimension is the ultimate stopping point for this round.

The Journey's Final Stretch

About 4,500 years ago, Earth's energetic vibration increased enough and needed a push to speed up the process. The last Ice Age had done a thorough job of cleansing, and life was slowly rebuilding. But the Negative Polarities were still around. They were tough to shake because no matter how often the Earth cleansed itself, the NPs found a way to regroup and restore their powers to stay in control. Each subsequent cycle had been a little more effective than the last, but the Earth's progression was far enough along that the NPs were getting worried and more aggressive. The Earth knew that the NPs' renewed push could damage the planet for good, so it called for help from the universal light brother and sisterhoods. In response, higher vibration Celestial Forces volunteered to come and increase the planet's energies by empowering Earth beings to lift their own. Celestial Forces are energy beings from other planets or elsewhere in the cosmos. They are "service-to-others" energies; their mission is to help increase energy vibration to return us all to "The One". Sometimes I refer to them as "Spirit".

This wasn't the first time the Celestial Forces offered to help. By Celestial Forces, I mean what some called "God", "Gods" or "Messengers". About 4,500 years ago, they approached ethnic groups, inviting them to live a higher vibrational life henceforth to help turn this around. They approached group after group, frightening some and turning off others. The beings had a tall order: Live more intentionally, thoughtfully and for the benefit of each other versus themselves. Many of their teachings were eventually organized into religions by the 3D humans, given that they are binary beings and understand things better through a structure.

Birth of Religions: To tell this story, I'll go back to that 4,500-year point (give or take) and march forward, showing you select milestones along the way to where we are in 2022. There may have been religions and activities before that date, but this is the earliest published date. This last stretch has been a vibrational speed-up considering how slow things were before the corner turn. As much as people complain about religion, it's played a vital role in hurrying this along. Yes, some people within a religion are still at the binary structural stage—do these ten things, and God will be happy, etc. But the systems have worked as planned, ushering many into a spiritual world and then turning them loose for self-exploration. A part of what's interesting about this is that religions emerged in different parts of the world around the same time—Central America, Indian subcontinent, Middle East, East Asia. Religions globally— indigenous and otherwise—universally report their beginning as stemming from invitations and instructions from one or more gods to move toward a higher vibrational way of life.

You'll notice that I do some light-touch dating throughout. I use dates as place-markers knowing that nothing can be accurately dated. We didn't even have a universal calendar until the 20th century, and many groups had their own systems and still do: kings, countries, regions, religious groups. Even the Jews have their own calendar. Often, many of the dates posited by these groups are thousands of years apart, making interpretation almost impossible. There's no way to pinpoint these events and no "proof" that something happened on a given date. We have no idea, for example, when Jesus was born. The calendar system we know today wasn't invented until long after Jesus reportedly left the Earth. Even then, not everyone accepted the newly-proposed dates. We're pretty sure that 25 December, the day it is currently celebrated, wasn't even close. The star constellation mentioned in the Bible at his birth put it sometime in the spring.

Many dates reported here came from carbon dating, geological and weather patterns, and oral traditions. Regardless, we have to start somewhere, so I'll place the events in chronological order based on what Western historians believe to be true so far. Of course, not all historians agree, but we must start somewhere.

The chronology I report is a reduction, for sure. There was far more going on than I can mention. It would take volumes to tell you everything, and I'm sure you don't want to read that much. I chose what I thought were the propelling highlights, focusing on extant religions among the thousands. My objective is to show a pattern versus write a comprehensive history. Some native traditions are missing from the list because they didn't leave behind written records. Native traditions tend to be passed by word of mouth, are decentralized, and are variable in their approach. Diasporas also erased memories.

Please note that the dates reported here are posited by the religion or the oldest date suggested by historians. I was after seed dates of when the Celestial Forces introduced Christ Consciousness. The list below gives you a rough-enough estimate of the creation of each religion to provide a timeline. Remember that most of these began as philosophies or spiritual practices and then evolved into religions by the 3D human leaders, creating dos and don'ts and lines in the sand. Some religions created sects to control the populace; others built theirs to lift the vibration. You will also see that the number of Gods decreases to one (or none) over time, a sign of a more advanced understanding of unity.

- Egyptian, est. 3200 BCE, multiple Gods
- Hindu, est. 3000 BCE, multiple Gods
- Jainism, est. 3000 BCE, no Gods
- Meditation, est. 3000 BCE, no Gods
- Yoga, est. 2700 BCE, no Gods
- Mayan, est. 2300 BCE, multiple Gods
- Minoan, est. 2000 BCE, multiple Gods
- Judaism, est. 1500 BCE, one God
- Zoroastrianism, est. 1500 BCE, one God
- Moses is born, 1391 BCE, one God
- Celtics, est. 1200 BCE, multiple Gods
- Buddhism, est. 500 BCE, no Gods
- Confucianism, est. 500 BCE, no Gods
- Birth of Jesus, est. 5 BCE, one God
- Tao/Dao, est. 140 CE, no Gods
- Christianity, est. 330 CE, one God
- Muhammad is born, 570 CE, one God
- Islam, est. 600 CE, one God
- Sikhism, est. 1500 CE, One God
- Shinto, est. 1800 CE, multiple Gods
- New Thought, est. 1830, no Gods
- Unitarian Universalist Humanism, est. 1960, no Gods

The list includes five benchmarks that aren't religions: meditation, yoga, and the births of Moses, Jesus and Muhammad. Each benchmark was a vital tool for vibrational lifting. Meditation and yoga are spiritual practices stemming from

Hindu philosophies. These practices are considered advanced and provide a more direct route to higher energy vibration. Today, they're practiced worldwide and have probably done more to lift Earth's vibration than other approaches.

Key Events: Growth in the world's population and increases in the Earth's vibrational energies led to a quickening of events bringing us closer to and more aware of ourselves and each other. Popular culture sees this as technological and economic growth, and that's true. But it misses the more significant changes behind it. Yes, tension came along with trying to stop the energy—that "yin, yang" thing never goes away. I don't include the pushbacks, only the events that raised energy vibration. What you'll notice is an ever-increasing number of tools to spread ideas and people. We tend to see those in economic or power terms, but the result of the efforts brought the world closer together and dismantled walls. This isn't a complete list, but it gives you an idea of movement and bubbling. I'll begin around the same time as previous timelines. You can add (in your mind) events you think are missing.

- 3000 BCE: Building of the Great Pyramid: A sign of spiritual development.
- 2500 BCE: Egyptians design ships to cross oceans: A tool to spread philosophies and trade.
- 753 BCE: Rome established: Ruled much of Europe, Israel and elsewhere for 600 years, spread Christianity.
- 500 BCE: Oldest extant candle used for illumination: Inside spaces can be lit; the God flame available in homes.
- 130 BCE: Silk Road begins: The first major expansion of world trade from China to Europe.
- 4 BCE: Wheel invented in Mesopotamia: Enabled vehicle travel and spreading of information.
- 29 CE: Crucifixion of Jesus: Hastened spread of Christ Consciousness.

- 1453 CE: Renaissance in Europe: The spread of art, music, theater, literature, industrialization.
- 1492 CE: Europeans (Columbus) claim North America, spreading global philosophies.
- 1498 CE: Sea-route to India discovered by Vasco da Gama: World ideas travel wide.
- 1600 CE: British East India Company established in India, exposing the British to Hinduism.
- 1776 CE: Declaration of American Independence: The USA is formed, spreading democracy.
- 1804 CE: Steam locomotive invented: Cross-country travel became easier and faster.
- 1837 CE: Electric telegraph invented: Enabled phone communication, allowing immediate communication across distances.
- 1861 CE: American Civil War begins: A fight for African American freedom and eventual uniting of the country.
- 1863 CE: Slavery legally abolished in USA: A human rights benchmark.
- 1869 CE: Opening of the Suez Canal for traffic: Worldwide trade expanded.
- 1886 CE: The gas engine invented: Individuals can now travel great distances more quickly.
- 1879 CE: Lightbulb invented: We can see in the dark more easily; public safety improved in urban areas.
- 1895 CE: X-Rays discovered: 3D medical personnel can see into the body to facilitate medical treatment.
- 1896 CE: Wireless invented: Spread of worldwide communications.
- 1905 CE: Theory of Relativity posited by Einstein: Expanded our knowledge of physics and united it with spirituality.
- 1919-20 CE: Treaty of Versailles signed, League of Nations Formed: The first signs of a path to worldwide peace.

- 1943 CE: Digital computer invented: Enabled data storage, computation and worldwide instant communication.
- 1945 CE: Hiroshima and Nagasaki experience the atom bomb: Destruction of the entire planet made possible and easy; spreads awareness of horror and a desire for worldwide peace.
- 1945 CE: United Nations formed: A lasting entity formed to bring world peace.

The Celestial Forces got to work after the atomic bombs were dropped and other countries raced to have their own. They realized that the bombs could quickly destroy the planet, and their proliferation had to be stopped. They'd had a long-term position of "help, but don't intervene", but they'd have to make an exception. "Enough is enough," they said. "We need to save this planet." So, they sent three waves of volunteers.

The Three Waves of Volunteers

What Are "Volunteers"? Three groups of advanced souls came to Earth in waves following World War II. The war's effect on the planet startled the Celestial Forces, and the volunteers came to "save the planet". To understand the war's influence and what happened to vibrational lifting, it's important to tell this story. The effect of the war had a more significant impact on Earth's vibrational evolution than any of the previous single events.

World War II Is the Call: The world percolated in pockets by the late 19th century, especially in Central Europe, where peace was forever fleeting (and still is). By 1914, tensions had risen in Central and Eastern Europe to the point that war broke out, creating a conflict involving countries beyond Europe. Philosophers, historians and politicians have called it World War I (WWI). The trigger was the murder of Archduke Franz

Ferdinand, the heir to Austro-Hungarian throne and his wife, the Duchess of Hohenberg. They were killed by Gavrilo Princip.

The war lasted until the end of 1918 and involved two powers: The "Central Powers" — Germany, Austria-Hungary, Bulgaria and the Ottoman Empire — fought against the "Allied Powers" — Great Britain, France, Russia, Italy, Romania, Japan and the USA. The additions of the latter two countries made it a world war. World War I saw unprecedented carnage and destruction (to date) thanks to new military technologies, especially airplanes dropping bombs from the sky. Over 16 million people died by the time it was over.

The war officially ended in June 1919 with the signing of the Treaty of Versailles, and the League of Nations was formed to bring countries together to live peacefully. However, there was a problem: The treaty's so-called "war guilt" clause forced Germany and other Central Powers to take all the blame for the war. This meant their loss of territories, reduced military forces and reparation payments to Allied powers. Germany grit its teeth, did it, and never forgave or gave up.

There was great prosperity in the USA, Canada and elsewhere in the Western world for the next ten years, ushering in "The Roaring Twenties". The era was a period of dramatic social and political change in the USA. For the first time, more Americans lived in cities than on farms. The nation's total wealth more than doubled between 1920 and 1929, and this economic growth swept many Americans into an affluent but unfamiliar "consumer society". Canada and the USA experienced relative peace at home.

The economy roared the loudest on the New York Stock Exchange. Share prices rose to unprecedented heights. The Dow Jones Industrial Average increased six-fold from 63 in August 1921 to 381 in September 1929. The world economy was also now profoundly laced with the American economy. Optimism was high.

Still, the rest of the world churned, including the Cristero War in Mexico, the Russian Revolution and the Chinese Civil War. In fact, during the decade, the world saw civil wars in 45 world regions.

The boom ended in an explosive bust. On Black Monday, 28 October 1929, the Dow declined nearly 13%. On Black Tuesday (the following day), the market dropped almost 12%. By mid-November, the Dow had lost almost half of its value. The slide continued through the summer of 1932, when the Dow closed at 41.22, its lowest value of the 20th century, 89% below its peak. "The Dow did not return to its pre-crash heights until November 1954," wrote Gary Richardson, Alejandro Komai, Michael Gou and Daniel Park in "Stock Market Crash of 1929". The article is published on the Federal Reserve website and dated 17 January 2022.

What happened? During the decade, the stock market peaked in August 1929 after a period of wild speculation. By then, production had already declined, and unemployment had risen, leaving stocks in significant excess of their actual value. Other causes include:

- low wages
- high debt
- a struggling agricultural sector
- an excess of large bank loans that could not be liquidated

By the end of October, the American economy was in ruins. The crash had crippled it because not only had individual investors put their money into stocks, but so did businesses, causing them to lose their money. Consumers also lost their money because many banks had invested it without their permission or knowledge. Many banks closed permanently; one out of four Americans were unemployed and without savings, and farm income fell by 50%.

The situation affected the rest of the world, especially Europe, which shared its prosperity with the USA. "The Great Depression" followed on both continents for the next decade. No part of Europe was untouched, albeit there were variations between countries. The worst affected countries were Poland, Germany and Austria, where one in five were unemployed and industrial output fell by over 40%. Levels of trade between countries also collapsed.

The Great Depression halted the German economy and further polarized German politics. Adolf Hitler and the Nazi party exploited the crisis, criticized the ruling government, and rose to power. The German Communist Party also began campaigning on the crisis and called for a revolution. Business leaders fearful of a communist takeover began supporting the Nazi party. In 1932 the Nazis held the most seats in the Reichstag, albeit short of an absolute majority. Eventually, Hitler became Chancellor in 1933 and later led the country to war, invading Poland in 1939. By 1941, Germany had regained its territory and spread into Western Europe.

I won't go deep into the war's history, but eventually, countries grouped again into sides and added other countries such as point: China, Japan, Cuba, Canada and others. The USA got involved after Japan attacked Pearl Harbor in 1941. Japan intended the attack as a preventive action. It aimed to prevent the USA Pacific Fleet from interfering with its planned military activities in Southeast Asia against overseas territories of the United Kingdom (UK), the Netherlands and the USA. On 7 December 1941, the USA declared war on Japan. Three days after Germany and Italy declared war on it, the USA became fully engaged in the Second World War. Of the players, the USA had the most extensive economic infrastructure, and millions of unemployed men enlisted immediately and entered with full force. The war revived the USA economy and brought the country together. Unfortunately, the war continued for four more years. Over 40 million people had died, which was 26% of the global population. There was no end in sight.

In 1945, the USA—specifically President Truman—quickly ended the war. He decided to drop two nuclear bombs on Japan in Hiroshima and Nagasaki, two of its largest cities.

The nuclear weapon is an explosive device that derives its destructive force from nuclear reactions. It releases large quantities of energy from relatively small amounts of matter, producing a fireball, shockwaves and intense radiation. A mushroom cloud forms from vaporized debris and disperses radioactive particles that fall to Earth, contaminating the air, soil, water and food supply. The fallout can travel thousands of miles and damage further away when carried by wind currents. Several nuclear explosions over a city such as New York, with its metropolitan area of over 20 million people, would wipe out the whole region and beyond in a few minutes. There would be no escape.

The bombing ended the war but also killed 220,000 more people. The devastation of the weapons, and the fact that other countries were building their nuclear arsenals, got the attention of the Celestial Forces. They saw that Earth was on a collision course with disaster. But what could they do? They couldn't directly interfere. So, they devised an alternative plan, deciding to influence things from the inside. The Celestial Forces sent out a call for volunteers to incarnate on Earth and help turn it around.

Dolores Cannon tells this story in her book *The Three Waves of Volunteers and the New Earth* (2011). Cannon (1931-2014) was a past-life regressionist and hypnotherapist specializing in recovering and cataloging lost knowledge. A retired Navy wife (her term) from Huntsville, Arkansas, Dolores was nearly 50 years old when she began experimenting with hypnosis and past-life regression. Her 20 books catalog what her clients reported on various topics, including the New Earth, extraterrestrial life, Jesus and the Essenes and others.

According to *The Three Waves*, Cannon noticed a pattern in her clients' reports. The Volunteers—Starseeds, Lightworkers and Wayshowers—arrived in three waves over 60 years, beginning with the war's end. A Volunteer is an incarnated entity who agreed to transmute the darkness into the light and, as a result, raise Earth's vibration. Cannon's clients said that the purpose was to increase the energy to avoid catastrophe and continue Earth's progress to a return to its 5D self.

The First Wave was born in the 1940s through the '60s and is known by some as Baby Boomers. The Boomers have had the most challenging time adjusting to 3D Earth. They arrived horrified by the hate, rampant violence, human slavery and lack of environmental care. Suicide rates have been higher in this group than in any other wave. Many First Wavers want to return home, even though they've forgotten home's location. All incarnated souls entered, having forgotten their past lives. To remember all of that would be overwhelming—the people they murdered, the starvation they experienced, etc. Disremembering is part of the karmic "re" incarnation system. As long as the Volunteer knows they have a peaceful purpose on Earth this time around, that's enough.

If needed, Volunteers can regain select memories through energy work, intuition therapy, astrology, meditation, etc. The information isn't lost: it's stored in the Akashic Records, which they can access when ready. The Akashic Records is an unlimited library of information housed in a higher vibrational dimension. Every thought, idea, and action from the past, present and future is stored there ad infinitum.

Each wave builds on the experiences of the next and has its characteristics. Characteristics bleed and overlap between the waves, of course, but the following serve as a basic guide. Also, note that every human born in each wave is not a Volunteer. Volunteers are a small, self-selected bunch.

First Wavers—born 1945 to 1969 (roughly)—tend to rebel against the status quo. Many have been the pioneers who paved the way for the second and third waves. First Wavers feel a burning need to save the world. They've fed the mental health movement, spread yoga and meditation, established nonprofits to take the "profit" out of helping others, protested wars, fought for civil rights, became energy healers, established animal sanctuaries, etc.

Second Wavers—born 1970 to 1985 (roughly)—transitioned to life on Earth more quickly than the First Wave. They work behind the scenes and often on their own, creating little or no karmic ripples. If they choose, they don't have to do anything; they can radiate their higher vibration to the world, affecting everyone near them. Many Second Wavers tend to be introverts and empaths. Introverts are people who prefer calm, minimally stimulating environments. They feel drained after socializing and enjoy solitude. Empaths are compassionate individuals with a keen ability to sense what people around them think and feel. Their purpose is to help the world lift its energy.

Third Wavers—born 1985-1999, roughly—arrived as the new hope of the world. Many came as exceptional children, with enhanced DNA compatible with a 5D vibration. Third Wavers need challenges to keep them interested. They can appear distracted and overly busy if they don't experience challenges. Unfortunately, Western medicine created a diagnosis for them, Attention Deficit and Hyperactivity Disorder (ADHD), which diluted the power for many. Most Third Wavers escaped the drugs, thankfully. Some Lightworkers call this wave "Indigo Children".

According to Gaia News, a respected curated source, an Indigo Child is an upgraded blueprint of humanity. This term came up when addressing the aura colors of these very different children. Previously, auric fields were expected rainbow shades, but a royal blue color dominated the Indigos' field. Thus, establishing a change of course in human evolution and their indigo aura. They are gifted children on a mission to challenge and shift reality. They are highly driven and creative, with a perception that sees through the established norms of society. Old souls indeed, their mission is laid out to shake up the modern world and pave the way for future generations to create greater peace and harmony for all.

Dolores reported three Waves, but there may be another. Fourth Wavers—2000-2015—is a category I created to represent what appears to be happening with today's children and youth, a group that wouldn't have undergone hypnosis with Dolores. Most are children and young adults, and we don't know a great deal about them. We do know, however, there has been an uptick in the number of vegans and vegetarians in this group, a stepping stone to lighten your vibration. I read daily social media posts from parents about their children saying that the youth don't want to eat meat anymore. The parents turn to Facebook pages for help, such as Vegan, plant-based and Vegetarian Recipes. The child's decision often moves the whole family to higher energy eating.

Since the First Wave, the ever-increasing vibrational energy has birthed several significant events and trends. I've selected some highlights by decade, concluding in the early 2020s when the book was submitted for publication. You'll notice that the examples represent spirituality, human rights (especially LGBTQ and I), technology and peace efforts in the USA. There's no uniform list, so I cobbled some events for illustration. I'm sure you're aware of many others.

Everything on this list is/was viewed as "bad" by some and "good" by others. These are neither "good" nor "bad". They are world event changes launching new waves of energy. They're pushing people to learn to be together. They help expose inequities, clear karma and launch new movements creating unity within diversity. With each launch, the Negative Polarities try even harder to restore their power. We aren't counting the "number" of things and keeping the score, putting "bad" on the left side of the balance and "good" on the right side. We're looking at trends and activities that bring people together and spread love and higher vibrations for a wider audience. One good thing can cancel 20 bad things.

Please note that because some decades have more events listed than others doesn't mean they were more important time periods. This isn't about the "number" of events in a decade because "number", a 3D phenomenon, has no registry in the cosmos. However, the end of World War II pushed so many emergency buttons that much happened quickly to set the new course. This isn't an exhaustive selection. Millions of events— large and small—were occurring, and you may know many more than what is listed.

In the 1950s:

- The United Nations opened in New York City, bringing countries together to solve common problems.
- The World Health Organization opens for business (1948, actually).
- Hawayo Hiromi Takata brings Reiki energy healing to the USA and begins teacher training.
- Television programming is widely available as an affordable learning tool.
- The DuMont Television Network expands on the UHF channel focusing on educational programming.
- The Mattachine Society becomes the first national gay rights organization.

In the 1960s:

- The music industry joins the Peace Movement with songs in the Top 40, e.g., Peter, Paul and Mary's *If I Had a Hammer*.
- Energy healing expands as a profession and professionalizes.
- A flood of Civil Rights laws is passed in the USA, including a law giving Blacks the right to vote.
- The Unitarian Universalist movement takes apart the Christian church and reorganizes it for self-examination.
- The Nuclear-Test-Ban Treaty is signed.
- The Public Broadcasting Act is passed.
- The Peace Corps is formed.
- *Born Free: A Lioness of Two Worlds* (and books like it) are published and become required reading in schools. The book by Joy Adamson describes her experiences raising a lion cub named Elsa and underscores the relationships between humans and animals. Novels discussing peace and love among all beings weren't new, but the format and style were different, and there were more of them.
- The Zen Center of Los Angeles is founded, spreading Japanese Zen meditation nationwide.

In the 1970s:

- The biggest increase in the number of nonprofit organizations in USA history.
- The mental health movement inspires publicly-funded counseling agencies, degree programs and professional certifications.
- LGBTQ and I communities organize into associations and "centers" to aid the community.

- Gay choruses join the community chorus world.
- Title IX gives women athletes the right to equal opportunity in school sports.

In the 1980s:

- AIDS, a catastrophic disease, teaches the acceptance of LGBTQ and I people and their relationships.
- Louise Hay, an American motivational author and the founder of Hay House, authors New Thought self-help books, including the 1984 book *You Can Heal Your Life*, creating a new genre and a publishing vehicle.
- Shumei America was founded, bringing a blend of Japanese Shinto and Buddhist philosophies to the USA per its founder Mokichi Okada.

In the 1990s:

- The Americans with Disabilities Act passed.
- The Family and Medical Leave Act was passed.
- Internet and wireless communication are available to all.
- Tony Kushner writes the play *Angels in America*, putting AIDS and Gay relationships in front of America on stage and screen. *Angels* opened a door for national marriage equality in 2013.

In the 2000s:

- The USA Supreme Court decision in Lawrence v. Texas declares a Texas statute that criminalizes same-sex sexual activity unconstitutional.
- Marriage equality for same-sex couples builds in the USA and other countries with legal recognition and protection.

- A concerted war protest effort forms in the USA with a series of global protests by 500,000 people.
- The Matthew Shepard and James Byrd, Jr. Hate Crimes Prevention Act becomes law in the USA.

In the 2010s:

- The Affordable Care Act goes into effect for millions of Americans, providing health insurance for the uninsured.
- The US Supreme Court affirms marriage equality, spreading worldwide.
- The USA and Cuba reestablish diplomatic relations after a 54-year lapse.
- Brexit happened: The UK (United Kingdom) leaves the European Union. Some saw this as a tragedy, but it was more an act of sovereignty and the right to individuality.
- Donald Trump is elected US President: This event, controversial with many people, broke many traditions into pieces worldwide. The breakages needed to happen to expose the Negative Polarity activities so that they could be seen and defeated. It was like shining a light on a problem: You can't solve it until you see it.

In the 2020s (2020–'22 Summer):

- COVID spreads worldwide, pushing people to relearn how to be together, work and build a new economic system. Interest in spirituality versus organized religion grows, too.
- Currency begins transitioning to virtual, and the total market cap of cryptocurrency passes USD 2 Trillion. Once seen as a speculative experiment, crypto became a monolith.

Chapter One

What Is Food?

Vibration as Food

Just as we did with energy and dimensions, we'll look at food from several angles. Third Dimension dictionaries define food as, "Any substance consumed to provide nutritional support for an organism. Food is usually of plant, animal or fungal origin and contains essential nutrients, such as carbohydrates, fats, proteins, vitamins or minerals." This definition is nutrition-based, treating our bodies as machines and food as fuel. Food, however, has two additional purposes: to raise our vibration and provide information.

I'll turn to the Lemurians to answer the "What is food" question from a vibrational and informational angle. Lemuria or Mu was a continent where heaven was a place on Earth, a 5D way of living. The Lemurians were a peaceful, highly intelligent race that existed millions of years ago. In Lemuria, life worked in harmony where all sentient beings were seen as equal; they were deeply respectful to Mother Earth. The Lemurians had a diet that maintained themselves and the planet's energy. These days, since the planet is returning to 5D vibrational energy, it would be helpful to see how their practices could help us. This chapter section also looks at plant versus animal foods as vibrational sources. We also visit honey.

The Lemurian Diet

The best source on the Lemurian diet is Magenta Pixie's *Lessons from a Living Lemuria: Balancing Karma through Nutrition for Ascension* (2020). I've read dozens of books on the Lemurians, but this one did the best job at summarizing the diet. Pixie is a UK channel for the higher dimensional, divine intelligence known as The White Winged Collective Consciousness of Nine. The Nine are a nonphysical, higher dimensional collective energy communicating with Pixie to make everyone aware of the light to raise everyone's consciousness and thus the planet by domino and 100th monkey effect.

The transmissions she receives from The Nine have reached hundreds of thousands worldwide via her video collection. Pixie has also published five books on ascension-related topics.

According to *Lessons*, the Lemurians have a vegan view on diet. I say "have" because many believe they are still with us in another dimension and that some live underground. Magenta asked The Nine, "What food should we eat to reach enlightenment and go through ascension?" In other words, how can we use food to raise our vibration?

The Nine responded:

There is no "should" here. Ascension has many stages, and one can move through an "ascension experience" regardless of dietary consumption. However, if one wishes to move through a fully aware ascension process in the most aligned way available to you at this time, which is that which we call "accelerated" or "stargate" ascension, one would need to have moved to that stage of mastery achieved by the indigenous peoples which is akin to being "karma-free". One needs to be as "light" as possible. The way forward here (if it is your calling and your desire) is to follow a predominantly vegan way of eating.

(Kindle Locations 154–160)

The book mentions the kinds of foods the Lemurians ate and why. I'll sprinkle some of them throughout the book. For example, the Lemurians ate mushrooms and pumpkins because of their extensive libraries of information. The Lemurians rarely ate fish, a 4D food. The point is that a vegan diet has the highest vibrational energy for ascension. Plant foods tend to be 3D to 5D in vibration compared to animal foods which are 2D to 3D.

So, why is the lower vibrational animal food problematic?

Animals as Food

Most conventional medical professionals prescribe animal products for dietary health. Some humans are wired for it as part of their karma. In fact, most are probably wired for it, so the medical professionals are partially correct. But because a medical doctor says "eat your meat" doesn't mean you have to do it. You might crave it, but you can get a healthier diet by eating vegan.

Most people know that eating plants is healthier, so many joke about it as they age. Here is some brief dialogue from a video I watched about a woman interviewed on her 100th birthday. The interviewer sat in a comfy chair, crossed his legs and asked, "To what do you attribute your longevity?" The woman smiled and pointed at him, "I eat bacon every day for breakfast." The answer was funny, but her longevity probably had more to do with general happiness and genetics. Actress Betty White made a similar joke when someone asked her the same question. "Don't eat any greens," she said. She'd thrown out the answer for a laugh, so we don't know if it was true, but it demonstrated her understanding that greens were important.

Humans with karma need to live as designed, learn the lessons and move on. They can't raise their vibration without learning. Sometimes those lessons are learned from eating meat, which sometimes takes millions of lifetimes. Maybe they need animal product messaging or the 2D/3D weightiness. Maybe they need to keep their vibration low in this round. They aren't ready to handle the higher vibrations. Each subsequent incarnation follows graduation from the first and builds on all prior incarnations. Once they've learned everything, they're one with the Universe.

The Problems with Animal Products

Eating animal products accidentally or occasionally poses little risk. Your body and Spirit can handle small doses just as your immune system handles stray germs. However, eating animal products with regular (or often) consumption can pose problems.

The first problem with animal products is that the animal's Spirit, DNA and life history are in the food. We are animals. Dogs are animals. Cows are animals. Animals are sentient beings with feelings, thoughts, intelligence, fears and karma. Fear and rage run through them and into every cell when they are killed for food. That, in turn, enters you when you consume the product cooked or raw. You can grill away some bacteria because they are lower in vibrational matter. But you can't grill away animal Spirit, a higher vibrational energy. Every bite of that steak has Animal Spirit in it, and after digesting it you now have bits of their karma, personality, joys and fears. You're not a cow, so you're not supposed to have all of that inside you. After integrating with your Spirit, theirs could disrupt your soul's journey. Theirs are theirs; yours are yours.

The second problem is the animal product's lower vibrational frequency. Nonhuman animal vibration is a 2D (sometimes 3D) vibration, and we want to reach 5D. If you eat lower vibrational foods, they integrate with yours and slow it down. Think of it as a Thanksgiving meal in which you overindulge to the point of sluggishness, where all that's left is to plop down in a comfy chair and watch a football game or a movie. Eventually, perhaps the next day, you'll come out of your food coma, but you won't come out of your lower vibrational coma if you consistently eat lower vibrational food. It will put you on the quicksand of a slower pace over time. These lower energies are also binary vibrations, reinforcing the idea within you that there is only one correct answer, one right race, one right religion, one right way to love, one correct gender, etc. If you see in and respond to the world in a black-and-white manner, even if you publicly verbalize otherwise, that reinforces the lower vibration and spills out and affects others. The "one right way" way of doing things holds you back. It feeds community division, violence, hate, poverty and world destruction on a grander scale. Of course, perhaps that's your karma, but if you're reading this book, I doubt that's your Spirit's plan.

The third problem is that animal products can build aggression within you. Animal consciousness includes aggressiveness and often sometimes turns violent. That formula works for animals, but it doesn't work for humans. This aspect of eating meat is why it is encouraged among soldiers and contact sports players. It's also why the term "red meat" means "aggression". Eating meat can build automatic aggressiveness so you can reflexively attack others and win.

There are differences in vibration in the kind of meat you eat. If you're trying to wean yourself from meat, move away from the lower vibrational meat and move toward the higher vibrational meat. Red meat has the lowest vibration (pork included); white meat is higher than red; fish is higher than white. Meats from four and two-legged creatures have 2D and sometimes 3D energies. Fish can have a 4D vibration, given their communal nature. Fish can serve as transition meat until you're ready to go entirely vegan.

Given the intention, eggs and dairy (especially dairy) have less animal Spirit than meat and a slightly higher vibration. That is because it's a residual with an intention: Milk is to feed a calf. It isn't actual flesh. Eggs, on the other hand, are meant to become another animal and are a "piece" of one and do not result in animal death. I lived on a farm. Chickens drop eggs all over the place and walk away from them. Those have a slightly higher vibration than the ones the chicken intuitively tries to hatch, knowing the egg will become a chick. A chick is growing inside it, and the mother's protection and love are part of their energy, but it's still a being. The intention is clear with eggs hatching under the mother's warmth: Those are not for food. Eggs to carry the parental psychologies, Spirit and karma.

Dairy has a slightly higher vibration because it's offered as a food to infant animals. It still carries the mother cow's karma, Spirit and DNA, but the intention of the supply raises the vibration. One big problem: It's food for a baby animal, not a human. It has a higher vibration for a baby cow than it would for you. Another problem is the processing source: Factory farms producing the milk often mistreat the mother cow and chemically induce milk production. The milk isn't freely offered under those conditions, which lowers its vibration. You'll also be consuming the chemicals.

It's up to you and your karma, of course. Even the Lemurians ate an occasional piece of fish, so you don't need to go binary about it. If your karma requires consumption of animal products, eat them. You'll have to listen to your intuition and body. Can you ascend eating meat? It's a "maybe yes, maybe no" answer depending on many factors, including your spiritual development. If your karma says, "Eat meat," you can still raise your vibration in other ways, including incorporating more plant foods into your diet. The Nine (and other entities) say that you won't reach "Stargate Ascension", which is the highest level, and that the ascension process could be longer and harder. Even Dolores Cannon reported her clients telling her that meat consumption slowed ascension. Your biggest problem is eating meat, but your karma says, "Plants only." In that case, you're not learning the lesson you're supposed to learn in this lifetime and may therefore be back for another. Ascension—the end of karma—may not be your intent this time.

Karmic Intent?

Understanding your karmic intent can come from many sources. You can access it independently through intuition, dreams, synchronicities, interests, skill sets, meditation, yoga and aha moments. You can also get help from astrologers, Akashic Record readers, psychics and card readers, and many other similar sources. DNA testing and genealogical research will also open doors. If your karmic lessons include not eating meat this time around, here are some 3D clues:

- if meat repulses you
- if your body is unhealthy
- if your mind (psychologically, spiritually, ethically, etc.) is unhealthy
- if you get repeated positive messages about vegan eating from medical professionals, family, friends, the media and others
- if one or more of your children go vegan

Honey as Nourishment

I began this journey seeing honey as an animal product and therefore avoiding it. I had a binary view of it: animal product, no consumption. Yet I kept bumping into honey's benefits for human use. For my allergy, a friend prescribed local honey. "Pollen is collected from flowers that believe they'll become a part of yet another thing that heals animals." I also read books and articles on spiritual nutrition mentioning honey's spiritual benefits and messaging. I stood my ground. But then a vegan friend had surgery, and her wound wasn't healing well. Her 3D conventional medical doctor recommended putting raw honey on the wound. My friend refused because she worried about contributing to the exploitation of bees. However, the surgery complications also concerned her, so she tried it and was quickly healed.

I realized that I'd been seeing honey through a binary lens, and binarism is a 3D filter, so I opened up my mind and heart. Yes, bees were living things and not plants. Yes, they made honey for their consumption. But honey is also a human healer, and it was also there for us. It's made from flowers, and those flowers understood that they'd become a part of a food that helped a variety of species—bees, humans and other animals. Flowers have a mission on the planet: Flowers bring a touch of eternity, joy and beauty which lie beyond the sorrows and cares of the human world. The bees bring that together for us in the form of a sweet nectar.

I understood that some commercial beekeepers harm bees, and I didn't want to contribute to their harm or incorporate their hurt in my body and energy. So, I was careful to buy honey from local beekeepers who respected bees. I purchased mine from a vendor at the Hollywood Farmers Market. I began periodically eating honey as a sweetener for my homemade plant ice cream (Nice Cream).

This book is about spiritual nutrition, not veganism, and honey has spiritual benefits for ascenders. You can leave honey alone. It's only one food. You don't have to eat every food on the list. If you're vegan to protect the animals and lift your vibration, and eating honey upsets you, don't eat it. There's no harm in it.

Plants as Nourishment

A big difference between plants and animals as food is the intention. Plants are alive and here for us; animals are alive, but they're here for themselves. Plants have nutrients and wisdom, too, and they provide oxygen for us to breathe. Without them, we couldn't survive. We're all aware of plant nutrients, but perhaps not their wisdom. I learned about this from several sources, and I list most of the sources in the Resources section under Plant Life. I mention a few examples of plant support below to give you a taste of what I mean. I will go into more depth in the next chapter.

Pumpkins hold a magical quality and can trigger subconscious awareness and knowledge of the shadow within humanity. This is why pumpkins are key Halloween symbols. They let you know what's hidden and can lead you to the truth. Cooked or raw, you get the information.

Coconut water has considerably more blue sapphire energy than other fruit liquids, although fruit liquids hold more than vegetable ones. Blue sapphire energy is higher vibration energy that includes spiritual insight.

"Wild blueberries are the most adaptable fruit on the planet," Anthony William wrote, "having survived drought, cold and floods. Hence, thousands of years of unique information are resting inside each plant—and no one berry is the same." His position was that if you ate wild blueberries, you ate their effort and drive, too, giving that "push through" stamina you need.

Ayahuasca is another source, but instead of eating it, you invite its Spirit to heal you through a shaman. A shaman has access to, and influence in, the world of spirits. The healing process is called "Plant Spirit Medicine". When people think of plant medicine, they understand it as a medicine brew made in a witch's black pot. But Plant Spirit Medicine is actually about engaging in a spiritual relationship with a living, highly-aware plant that wants to help. Plant Spirit Medicine helps balance the subtle inner elements to flourish our health, mind and spiritual development.

Plant Feelings and Communication

Animals are alive. Plants are alive. Animals are sentient. Plants are not sentient. Animals have feelings, but do plants? When you eat a killed sentient being, you eat their emotions, including the pain magnified by the death. But is there any pain to the plant when you kill it? Is yanking an apple off the tree the same as yanking a baby calf from its mother eating it as veal?

The argument I usually get from omnivores confronting me about not wanting to kill an animal to eat it is that if it's wrong to kill animals, it's wrong to kill plants. The Lightworker community doesn't argue that it's wrong to kill, in general, but there isn't a single human being on Earth that doesn't kill to survive: The front of our car kills insects as we drive. Twenty-seven states legally kill convicted criminals. Even our body destroys itself: Our cells die off every seven years and are replaced with new ones. The issue isn't "do not kill", the issue is the energy we're eating and how it affects our vibration.

I mentioned earlier that sentient beings have feelings, but do plants? And if they do, don't we incorporate those feelings into us when we eat them? The answer is a "yes, but".

Plants have feelings, but a feeling to a plant isn't the same as it is for an animal. There are two reasons for this. First, plant intelligence is diffused across the species; animal intelligence is concentrated in the brain. The brain processes almost everything for the animal being. It takes in information, analyzes it, makes decisions based on it, remembers it, etc. The brain isn't the sole processor, of course. Other parts of the animal's body have similar functions; the entire body stores memories, given that DNA is memory and DNA is in every cell. But the brain is the decider that "informs" the rest of the body.

Putting everything into one place, such as a brain, limits and intensifies things. It's like putting all of your money into a single stock. If the stock does well, hurrah! If it crashes, you crash with it. It's all or nothing. It's the same with an animal. The crash is stored throughout the body. When you eat the animal, you eat the crash, and it becomes a part of you.

Plants don't have this brain-thing; they are communal, not singular units. In the animal world, the animal is the unit.

The being in that body is gone when the being dies. Plants function as a species; the plant in front of you isn't "the plant" like the human in front of you is "the human". It's a single molecule within an entire species. When you take pull onions from the ground, there are plenty others that carry on as if nothing happened.

A significant reason for the difference is purpose. Animals and plants process feelings differently because they're here for different reasons. An animal is a 2D or 3D creature with a primarily service-to-self mission. Most plants, however, bend toward the 4D and 5D frequencies and have a service-to-others purpose. Plants are here to show beauty, to make us feel good, to remove carbon dioxide from the air, and convert it to oxygen for our breathing. Plants are here to feed us, too:

- apples and seeds fall from the tree
- dark leafy greens give us vital nutrients
- plants provide fiber to clean out our internal systems

Plants rejoice when we rely on them. Sure, some may have an initial feeling of surprise, but that's temporary and has no long-lasting effect. Let's turn to science for evidence of the physical piece.

One of the most comprehensive texts on plant life is Stefano Mancuso's *Brilliant Green* (2015). Mancuso reviewed and summarized plant research going back 150+ years to Charles Darwin. Mancuso is the director of the International Laboratory of Plant Neurobiology in Florence, Italy. He posits that having intelligence in animals and plants is a prerequisite for experiencing feelings, and plants have intelligence. Plant intelligence is formed and expressed differently from animals, however. "Today's view of intelligence," he wrote, "as the product of the brain in the same way that urine is of the kidneys, is a huge oversimplification." He adds that the plant's brain isn't a single organ, nor is it centrally located. Intelligence is in every cell, with the root tips being the most sensitive receptors. The entire network is a vast, single plant intelligence for a rhizome plant.

A rhizome is a stem that grows underground, usually horizontally. Since it's a stem, it has nodes and can put out other stems, usually straight up and above ground. This means a patch of what looks like several individual plants grouped near each other may actually be shoots of the same plant, put up by the same rhizome. Examples include mint, bamboo and poison ivy. I had several stories from childhood when my maternal grandmother asked me to help her out by "digging out of all the mint creeping into her hedge". That was tough to do. If I pulled out one, others came out with it, which was good except I could see roots all over the place underground, sending the signal that this was hopeless. They'd grow back, and they always did. I swear they grew back more challenging for the next round of weeding.

Rhizome networks can be extensive. Pando, thought to be the world's most giant living thing by mass, is a forest in Utah of 47,000 aspen trees that come from a single root system. Panda spreads over 106 acres in Utah, making it genetically one plant.

Dr. Jon Lieff, MD, had similar findings as Mancuso. His model also demonstrates how plants communicate holistically. Dr. Lieff is a practicing psychiatrist and a graduate of Harvard Medical School. He has a blog titled *Intelligent Cells Know Their Place* (29 March 2015). He discussed how the body healed through cell communication and then compared it to plants in a post. According to Lieff, plants consist of cells like humans, and he created a model based on research to describe how they think and communicate. "By following multiple rules and measurements and synthesizing this information, cells can calculate where they are," he said.

There are many possible sources of error that must be considered. Cells use data from different sources such as morphogenic fields of diffusible molecules, electrical gradients and complex genome networks. Recent research shows that as well as being able to calculate many different factors and taking them into account, cells are, at the same time, signaling back and forth to other cells, sharing information that helps determine the exact location.

With cell intelligence comes feelings. Nicoletta Lanese in *LiveScience* published an article titled "Plants 'Scream' in the Face of Stress" (6 December 2019), suggesting that plants stressed by drought or physical damage emit ultrasonic squeals. In times of stress, people sometimes let out their angst with a squeal, and Lanese reported something similar for plants. "Unlike human screams, however, plant sounds are too high-frequency for us to hear them, according to the research... But when researchers from Tel Aviv University in Israel placed microphones near stressed tomato and tobacco plants, the instruments picked up the crops' ultrasonic squeals from about four inches (ten centimeters) away." The authors noted, "The noises fell within a range of 20 to 100 kilohertz, a volume that could feasibly be detected by some organisms from up to several meters away."

In another experiment reported in Ananas Esperide's *The Music of the Plants* (2014), Cleve Backster, an ex-CIA agent and an expert in using lie detectors, reported similar results. He connected his dracaena, a spike-leafed tropical houseplant, to a galvanometer "and noticed that the plant reacted with exceptional electrical activity to various stimuli, as if it could perceive them and chose how to react to them." Backster and his colleagues connected hundreds of different plant species to the device and showed that the plants responded to circumstances around them, even across species. The plants abhorred interspecies violence: "When a shrimp was put into boiling water, alive, the electrical signals from the plants peaked, almost as if they had 'fainted' from the shock."

These findings and models are from contemporary times, but we've known about plant intelligence for at least 150 years, thanks to Charles Darwin (1809-1882). Darwin was an English naturalist, geologist and biologist, best known for his contributions to the science of evolution. He'd made many other findings that weren't accepted well. His theory of plant intelligence didn't get the traction of evolution, and poor Darwin didn't have a website or a social media platform to advance his beliefs. However, his findings were (are) known in scientific circles to this day, and that's how they made it to this page. They didn't make it into high school textbooks.

Charles Darwin may have been the first who noted plant abilities to communicate with their environment (Darwin 1880). He showed that plants generate specially shaped sexual organs (his term) that allow insects and birds to access their flowers. Plants reward these pollinators with nectar and other compounds, which are both attractive and a necessary part of the diet of these insect/bird feeders. These plants are thus masters of a deceptive and intelligent strategy for their own reproduction, using insects and birds to spread their seeds.

Plant communication also moves through a communal source of a network of plants of the same and different species. The study "Aboveground Mechanical Stimuli Affect Belowground Plant-plant Communication" (*PLos One*, 2018) supports this notion. According to the study, plants use their roots to "listen in" on their neighbors. Plants living in a crowded environment secrete chemicals into the soil that prompt their neighbors to grow more aggressively, presumably to avoid being left in the shade. The study focused on corn seedlings, which boost growth in a stressed environment. Velemir Ninkovic, the lead researcher, and an ecologist at the Swedish University of Agricultural Sciences in Uppsala, simulated the touch of a nearby plant by stroking the leaves for a minute each day using a makeup brush. When his team removed the plant and placed a new one in its growth solution, the plant diverted its resources to grow more leaves and fewer roots. Seedlings planted in growth solutions that had previously hosted untouched plants did not show this pattern.

"If we have a problem with our neighbors, we can move flat," Ninkovic said. "Plants can't do that. They've accepted it, and they use signals to avoid competing situations and to prepare for future competition."

Plants have no central nervous system, so they can't "feel" like an animal can feel. They do, however, have a consciousness, and it may be that consciousness that reacts as fear. We turn to that next.

The Plant Personality

Earlier, I mentioned Plant Spirit Medicine that works with the "spirit" of the plant and not always the physical plant. They call for the spirit just as a channeler might channel a being, or a Reiki Master might bring forth energy. Most plants are here to heal us in one way or another, but select plant species have healing missions. Each plant—or plant species—has a purpose, but Shamans and spirit guides know which to call on to heal and which to leave alone.

I honed this idea while reading Anthony William's work, *Medical Medium* (2015). William has a unique ability to converse with what he called the "Spirit of Compassion". Spirit of Compassion gave him the gift of reading people's conditions and telling them how to recover their health. His advice includes all kinds of self-care, from believing in yourself to eating a vegan diet. William's book helped me see beyond the nutrients and into what else the plant had to offer. I knew that plants had Spirit within them, but I didn't think the Spirit part affected us. I thought you had to call up Spirit for help. I didn't realize that I could eat plant spirit and have it incorporated within me. I knew that animal spirit did that, but not plant.

William wrote that plants had personalities and histories, and that eating them incorporated everything into you. His discussion on wild blueberries helped me see it.

Wild blueberries hold ancient and sacred survival information from the heavens, going back tens of thousands of years. They have adapted to every fluctuation in climate over the millennia. Their innate intelligence has prevented them from accepting a monoculture; instead, they thrive with more than 100 variable strains that look similar yet have different genetic makeups, so that these plants can never be eradicated, no matter what comes in the future.

He offered similar explanations for every plant he suggested we eat. By the time I finished the book, I'd turned 180 degrees on plant understanding and personified them. I saw plants not only as living things but with an "aliveness" inside that could lift me by eating them. Eating plants was like eating animals: What was ever inside them—nutrients, personality characteristics, histories—came inside you during digestion. Except with plants, I could get healing energy from them without incorporating their fear, karma or diseases.

Later, I went on a spiritual retreat in Crestone, Colorado, and learned more about how this worked. Crestone is a four-hour drive southwest of Denver and far from any urban civilization. It sits 7,500 feet in elevation and is ringed on three sides by mountains. An array of two dozen or more retreat centers and sacred landmarks are south of the town's center, including ashrams, monasteries, temples, retreat centers, stupas, labyrinths and sacred landmarks. It's a spiritual mecca, and the energy is mellow and clear.

I attended a five-day retreat for Shinji Shumeikai (Shumei) members. The event was held at their multi-acre retreat center nestled into the hills. Shumei is a spiritual fellowship based outside of Kyoto, Japan, with satellites worldwide, including two in Los Angeles and others across the country. The organization fosters health, happiness and harmony for all by applying the spiritual leader's wisdom and insights, Mokichi Okada. Its philosophies and spiritual practices are a blend of Buddhism and Shintoism. I am a long-term member.

A forest hike was planned, during which we self-divided into two groups of eight based on our hiking stamina. I chose the higher stamina group, which just happened to be the right group to learn about singing plants. The hired group leader was an expert.

After my group reached the top of our rocky climb, we stopped for a breath. Everyone gathered in a small circle, and Peter, the group leader, pulled out his cell phone. I thought it was odd because I was sure there was no signal this deep into the forest.

Peter was a middle-aged lad with dishwater blonde hair and an intentional, boy-exploring look. He was also a professional musician who, it turned out, saw plants as vocal instruments. We were in his element, and I'd be soaking everything up.

"Do you want to hear the plants sing?" Peter said.

"Sing?" I asked. Plants sing? How could plants sing? They didn't have brains or vocal cords.

Peter adjusted the settings on the screen, and an etheric space-age sound came out of it. "Here's a (something or another plant) singing," he said. "I recorded it using this." He pulled out a bamboo-jacketed device from his pocket the size of a transistor radio from the '60s. "It has wires that you plug into it, and you hook the wires to the plant. One wire goes to a leaf, and the other goes into the ground to touch a root. The device picks up the electrical currents moving through the plant and converts them to sound. The currents are communication. Plants understand each other, but this device converts the communication into something audible so we can hear them."

We passed the phone around the circle and listened. The others listened for five to ten seconds and then passed it on like a hot potato. Fortunately, I was last. I took the phone and listened, and I couldn't let it go. The plant was speaking to me. It wasn't using words, yet I could understand its feelings by the punctuation, flow, pitches and modes it chose. Goosebumps grew all over me.

"What you're hearing is plant communication," Peter said.

I finally found the coordination to open my mouth. "Where did you get the device?"

"Damanhur," he said.

"A place or a store?"

"A place."

The other group members bit their lips and tapped their toes, hoping I'd quit asking questions. I felt the pressure, so I stopped. While hiking down the hill, I wondered where Damanhur was and how someone knew to invent this thing? I waited until we finished the walk and cornered Peter. He seemed busy, so I got his card and asked for the correct spelling of Damanhur.

That night online, I researched Damanhur and plant singing. Damanhur was a Federation of spiritual communities in Northern Italy with a constitution, culture, art, music, currency, schools and advanced science and technology. Its citizens were open to sharing their knowledge and research with other groups and cultures of the world with anyone interested in exploring these themes. They'd invented the plant recording device, and I could get it from one of their American distributors. I called the following day and ordered it. I wanted to hear what plants had to say and to understand it. I wanted to learn plant language.

From these episodes — Mancuso's and William's books, Plant Spirit Medicine, the Shumei retreat and other experiences — I went from seeing plants from a purely nutritional perspective to spiritual, vibrational and quasi-human perspectives. I saw myself — all of us — in partnership with these plants to build ourselves and everything around us. Once I equalized the spirit potential of plants and animals, I saw more clearly why I should be petting animals, not eating them.

Chapter Two

The Spiritual History of Eating

Overview

This chapter is about ushering out the old patterns to make room for the new. If we think about eating in a spiritual sense, many of us think of the suggestions and rules of our childhood religions. Even if you were raised in a moderately religious environment—you went to temple or church on major holidays, baptized the children, put your religion on application forms when asked—the religion may have influenced you without realizing it. If you did know it and later rejected it, there may be lurking ancestral memories of these practices. Before you learn spiritual nutrition tools, it would be a good idea to shine a flashlight on the old religious tapes so you can see them. Once you see them, they are easier to set aside (if you choose).

In this chapter, I unpack some religious dietary practices. If you weren't raised in a religion, this information is still valuable for understanding your friends', family members', coworkers' and neighbors' practices and beliefs. To ease discussion, I group the religions into three categories and discuss them alphabetically: Abrahamic, Eastern and Mesoamerican. Please remember that some of the Eastern religions aren't considered religions by many scholars and adherents. They are considered philosophies, especially the Eastern practices of Buddhism, Confucianism and Tao. Even Judaism isn't considered a religion by some Jews. Most Jews see themselves as a nation, and many see themselves as a race. There are also nonpracticing ethnic Jews, especially in Western Europe and the USA. In the States, they call themselves "Cultural Jews". Regardless, I employed reductionism to enable a discussion. Sometimes, you have no choice.

Before I begin, I want to provide a second disclaimer. Yes, I have a PhD in Public History, but it centers on the Renaissance period in the UK, not world religions. The degree covered European religious practices at the time, but not world religions. However, the terminal degree taught me to conduct and analyze research, which I did on these pages. Please note that my findings may differ from your understandings. I had to again tap reductionist summarization to find a central meaning, a challenge given the conflicting views among practitioners and scholars.

Regardless, I intend to illustrate how ancestral thoughts impact diet. This isn't an exhaustive overview, but it's enough. Thank you for understanding.

The Abrahamic Religions

The Abrahamic religions are a group of Semitic-originated religious faith communities claiming descent from the Judaism of the ancient Israelites and worshiping the God who spoke to Abraham. Semitic means relating to the peoples who speak/spoke Semitic languages, especially Hebrew and Arabic. Judaism, Islam and Christianity are the three most common Abrahamic religions. Those three combined have the most significant number of adherents on Earth.

Before we begin, please note that there is no primary source or period-specific evidence that any of the patriarch-founders existed. We know about them from the reports of others. A primary source is some form of notation from the public records or written communications from the individual. There are also no period secondary sources. Secondary sources include the writings of others from the period or later. These religions operate on faith that the patriarchs existed, and nothing is wrong when you believe it. Perhaps they lived, and the later sources were correct. We don't need physical proof; it's the beliefs carried forth that matter. Those beliefs come to us in various ways that aren't quantifiable.

Abrahamic, a term derived from the patriarch Abraham, describes monotheistic religions, meaning that the followers believe in only one God. Abraham is a central biblical figure.

I have ancestry and appreciation for all three Abrahamic traditions. I am Jewish (with proof). I grew up Christian. My maternal grandmother is ancestrally Islamic. I have affection, appreciation and good feelings for all three.

The Abrahamic religious texts mention eating meat and provide guidelines for safely choosing and preparing it in some cases. For Jews, the God narrator established the guidelines for the great flood. Noah's family, on the boat in need of food, needed help from above. Plant life was now submerged, and they could only find animals to eat—fish, birds. Eating animals came with health dangers, so God the narrator established guidelines.

I will briefly describe each religion and present its dietary rules and/or guidelines.

Christianity: Christianity is a religion founded about 1,900 years ago based on the reported life and teachings of Jesus of Nazareth, a Jew. Christianity is the world's largest religion, with an estimated 2.4+ billion followers. Its adherents, known as Christians, believe that Jesus is the Christ, the Son of God, the savior of all people, and the Messiah prophesied by the Jewish people. The Christian *Bible* (as opposed to the Hebrew *Bible*) is the main text, divided into Old and New Testaments. The Old Testament consists of much of the Jewish *Tanakh* but with edits, deletions and additions. The New Testament is the principal guide for Christians. Many Christians view the Old Testament as history and philosophy, albeit there are differences of opinion on this depending on the denomination.

Jesus' work as an adult is chronicled in the New Testament 100 hundred years after his death by his disciples. These "books" mention nothing about diet except to describe what people ate. The Old Testament had dietary laws, but most Christians don't see them as applying to them.

The most significant reference to food is in the story of the Last Supper mentioned in four places in the New Testament: Matthew 26:17-29; Mark 14:12-25; Luke 22:7-38; and 1 Corinthians 11:23-25. According to Christian scripture, taking Communion originated at the Last Supper. Jesus was said to have passed unleavened bread and wine around the table and explained to his Apostles that they represented his body and blood.

Another food reference is Jesus' second miracle, reported in Matthew 15:32-39 and Mark 8:1-9. Jesus reportedly fed 4,000 people with seven loaves of bread and a few small fish.

What do Christians understand and practice beyond Communion and imitating elements of the Last Supper? It varies. At least one Christian denomination recommends vegetarianism: The Seventh-day Adventists. They posit:

Exercise and avoidance of harmful substances such as tobacco, alcohol and mind-altering substances lead to clear minds and wise choices. A well-balanced vegetarian diet that avoids the consumption of meat coupled with intake of legumes, whole grains, nuts, fruits and vegetables, along with a source of vitamin B12, will promote vigorous health.

Members of the Seventh-day Adventist Church have promoted variations of the Seventh-day Adventist diet since the church's inception in 1863. They believe their bodies are holy temples and should be fed the healthiest foods. The dietary pattern is based on the biblical Book of Leviticus (Old Testament) in which meat-eating guidelines are set. That chapter provides guidelines for selection, preparation and presentation.

About a third of the denomination's members practice either vegetarianism or veganism.

Islam: Islam teaches that there is only one God (Arabic: Allah) and that Muhammad is the messenger of God. Islam is the world's second-largest religion, with over 1.8 billion followers, most known as Muslims. The religion teaches that God is merciful, all-powerful and unique and has guided person-kind through prophets who revealed scriptures and natural signs. The *Quran* is the central religious text of Islam, which Muslims believe to be Allah's revelation.

Islam has dietary laws framed by the understandings of halal and haram. Halal is permitted food; haram food is not permitted. Permitted foods include all fruits, vegetables, lentils and grains. Permitted meat has limits, however. The 2 *Quran* 173 states, "Indeed, what he has forbidden for you is the flesh of dead animals." Many interpretations of this include that if the animal is found dead, you can't eat it. If it's found alive, you can kill it to eat it. It's also haram to consume flowing blood and the flesh of swine. Animals dedicated to anyone but Allah are also haram.

Many groups forbid alcohol, but other interpretations and exceptions are scattered throughout. Regarding fish, "Its water is pure, and its dead are halal to eat."

Judaism: Many believe that Judaism is the world's oldest monotheistic religion. Judaism is characterized by a belief in one transcendent God who revealed himself to Abraham, Moses and the Hebrew prophets, and a religious life per scriptures and rabbinic traditions. Judaism is the complex phenomenon of a total way of life for the Jewish people, comprising theology, law, geography and cultural traditions.

The *Torah* is the final word on Jewish law and tradition; it is
also incorporated into the Christian Old Testament. *Torah* is the
Jewish Nation's Constitution and has plenty to say about diet.
The book of Genesis begins by defining plants as the source of
food:

*And God said, let the earth bring forth grass, the herb yielding
seed, and the fruit tree yielding fruit after his kind, whose seed is
in itself, upon the earth: and it was so. And the earth brought forth
grass, and herb yielding seed after his kind, and the tree yielding
fruit, whose seed was in itself, after his kind: and God saw that it
was good.*
Genesis 1:11–12

And,

*God said, "See, I give you every seed-bearing plant that is upon all
the earth, and every tree that has seed-bearing fruit; they shall be
yours for food."*
Genesis 1:29

Notice that only plants are mentioned as food. Meat is
referenced in 10 Genesis only after the flood when all plant
life is submerged. Of course, the people on Noah's ark had to
eat something, so an exception was made with guidelines. The
Genesis flood story (chapters 6-9) is the Hebrew version of the
universal flood archetype. It tells of God's decision to return
the universe to its pre-creation state.

Later, in the book of Leviticus, there's a list of "clean" and
"unclean" foods for its Levite priests. The foods presented
were considered part of an exemplary diet worthy of serving
in the Temple. Again, safe to eat meats are listed. The guides

like telling folks, "Hey, if you have to drink booze, could you at least drink 3.2 beer?" Forbidden meats included predatory birds and animals, and most insects and animals that do not have cloven hooves or that chew their cud.

For Jews, the list in Leviticus falls within the definition of "kosher". Kosher provides rules for meat selection, preparation and consumption. Kosher is about more than the Jewish diet, however: It means "according to the requirements of Jewish law." A kosher mikvah, for example, is an immersion in water derived from a natural source such as a river or a lake, a procedure spelled out in the *Torah*. Kosher speech means the words are kind and uplifting.

As of 2020, Israel had the second-highest percentage of vegetarians globally—13%. Many Jews take the introductory lines in Genesis to heart.

The Eastern Religions

The Eastern religions are a vast span of beliefs understood across much of Central and East Asia. For the sake of brevity, I chose seven of the most widely known: Buddhism, Confucianism, Tao, Hindu, Jain, Shinto and Sikh.

Eastern philosophy has more to say about eating and spirituality than Western. Adherents also tend to lean vegetarian and vegan.

Again, please note that there is no primary source or period-specific evidence that any of the patriarch-founders existed. They may have lived, and it's okay to believe they did, but there is much similarity about how they emerged as spiritual leaders and what they taught. They may be archetypes.

Buddhism: Buddhist philosophy encompasses various traditions, beliefs and spiritual practices primarily based on original teachings attributed to Siddhartha Gautama.

Gautama, called The Buddha (a title), was a monk, mendicant, sage, philosopher, teacher and spiritual leader from present-day Nepal. Buddhism has an estimated 520 million followers worldwide and is the fourth most practiced religion in the world behind Hinduism. But for many—including me—Buddhism is a philosophy versus a religion.

The philosophy originated sometime between the 6th and 4th centuries BCE (Before the Common Era) and has developed into three main branches: Theravada, Mahayana and Vajrayana. There are no Gods, but all three branches share the common goal of overcoming suffering and the cycle of death and rebirth, albeit they vary on how to get there. All three tend to agree on a list of Precepts meant as philosophical reflections versus commandments or laws. Keeping the precepts is a discipline that helps Buddhists live harmoniously with others while learning to actualize the Buddha's teachings. Dietary beliefs and practices stem from the Precepts.

The Precept most frequently referenced when discussing diet is the First Grave Precept: "Do not kill." Many understand it as referencing sentient beings, but it actually refers to any form of life, ideas, or even happy thoughts. It stems from a natural need to not hurt others because hurting someone (or something) can create karmic ripples causing collateral damage, including to oneself. When you hurt one thing, you hurt everything. In Buddhism, everything is one thing.

The Dalai Lama, the head of Tibetan Buddhism, is vegetarian, and many scholars believe that The Buddha was also a vegetarian. However, stories tell us that The Buddha accepted meat under two conditions:

1. as a gift from a host at a meal
2. as an offering to him as a mendicant (accepting the meat in appreciation)

If you eat meat as a gift, he recommended thanking the animal for its life and for nourishing your body. Gratitude helps mitigate the harm of killing.

The precepts are paths and not fundamental laws, so each branch of Buddhism has diet variations. Theravada Buddhists are more inclined to believe that eating meat is okay if the animal isn't killed on your behalf. Many Mahayana Buddhists believe that killing any sentient being is wrong. Vajrayana practitioners eat meat.

Confucianism: Confucianism is based on Confucius' teachings. Confucius (the Latinized name of K'ung Fu-tzu) was a Chinese teacher and philosopher. He was born in 551 BCE in Qufu, a city in Shandong, an eastern province on the Yellow Sea known for its Taoist and Confucian heritage. The philosophy played an important role in forming Chinese character, behavior and way of living. The philosophy posits achieving harmony, the most important social value. Confucianism emphasizes mercy, social order and fulfillment of responsibilities. People accomplish this through well-defined roles and appropriate actions towards others.

Its central ethical principle, "Ren", is equivalent to the concepts of love, mercy and humanity. The direction is taken from Confucius' statement, "Do not do to others what you do not want done to yourself." Confucian philosophy believes that food and friends are inseparable parts of life. A life without food and friends is considered incomplete and improper.

Confucian philosophy cautions us from eating meat. It also has this to say about eating:

- food should be served in small or chopped pieces
- the taste of any dish depends on proper mixing of all of its ingredients and condiments

- taste of individual elements does not have great importance in food, but fine blending of ingredients results in great taste, and dishes in meals must be compatible
- blending of food also results in harmony and is an important part of the philosophy; without harmony, foods cannot taste good
- eat only at mealtimes
- don't eat food that smells bad
- don't consume food that is not well cooked
- eat fresh and local; do not eat food out of season
- don't eat when the sauces and seasonings are not correctly prepared
- eat ginger but in moderation to not increase the internal heat of the body
- know the origin or source of your food
- the way you cut your food reflects the way you live
- eat meat only in moderation
- eat only until seven-tenths full; control in portions promotes longevity
- you need not limit drinking, but do not drink to the point of confusion
- hygiene is essential in food preparation

I always chuckle when I read the guideline on drinking. I think Confucius wanted to say, "Do not drink, period," but understood that if he said that, folks would revolt and then ignore all of the guidelines.

Hinduism: Hinduism is an Indian religion and dharma or way of life comprised of religious, cultural and philosophical concepts. It is widely practiced in the Indian subcontinent and parts of Southeast Asia and is the world's third-largest religion, with over 1.25 billion followers or 15-16%. Most scholars believe Hinduism started somewhere between 2300 BCE and 1500 BCE.

The Hindu concept of God is manifold. Hindus believe that one primary, omniscient and omnipotent deity is called Brahma. Hundreds of thousands of other deities represent particular facets of the all-knowing, absolute and primary Brahman. Primary scriptures include the *Vedas* and *Upanishads*, the *Bhagavad Gita*, the *Ramayana* and the *Āgamas*.

Hinduism does not require a vegetarian diet, but many Hindus avoid meat because they don't want to hurt other life forms. Vegetarianism is considered sattvic. A sattvic diet is a regimen that emphasizes seasonal foods, fruits, dairy products, nuts, seeds, oils, ripe vegetables, legumes, whole grains and non-meat-based proteins. In modern literature, a sattvic diet is sometimes referred to as a yogic diet. Hindus believe that diet purifies the energy in your body.

Hinduism's history, development and the locus of its adherents are in India. India has the highest percentage of vegetarian residents at 38%.

Jainism: Jainism is an ancient Indian religion. The premises are ahiṃsā (non-violence), anekāntavāda (many-sidedness), aparigraha (non-attachment) and asceticism. These premises have led to a predominantly vegetarian lifestyle among Jains that avoid harming animals and their life cycles. The Jains also encourage eating very little food.

Shinto: Shinto is a native religion in Japan and remains unique to the country. It includes numerous folk beliefs in deities and spirits. Practices include divination, spirit possession and shamanic healing. Shinto is about celebrating human life and kami, also known as gods manifesting themselves in various forms like rocks. The Four Affirmations of Shinto are as follows:

- tradition and the family: understanding that family is the foundation for preserving traditions

- love of nature; holding nature sacred
- ritual purity; ritual bathing to cleanse yourselves spiritually and physically before entering a shrine to worship the kami
- matsuri: worshipping and honoring gods and ancestral spirits

Shinto's influence on diet is the practice of purity, an important aspect of the religion. Initially, Shintoism frowned on eating meat because it made the body impure. After WWII, however, the country opened and adopted some Western practices. Today, under 5% of the Japanese are vegetarians.

Anecdotally, my Japanese friends tell me that incidences of cancer and heart disease have risen as a result of meat eating.

Sikhism: Sikhism coming from the word Sikh, meaning a "disciple", "seeker" or "learner". Sikhism is a monotheistic religion that originated in the Punjab region in the northern part of the Indian subcontinent around the end of the 15th century CE (Common Era). It is one of the youngest of the major world religions and the world's fifth-largest in terms of adherents. The fundamental beliefs of Sikhism, articulated in the sacred scripture *Guru Granth Sahib*, include:

- faith and meditation on the name of the one creator
- divine unity and equality of all humankind
- engaging in selfless service
- striving for justice for the benefit and prosperity of all
- honest conduct and livelihood while living a householder's life

Only lacto-vegetarian food is served in the Gurdwara (Sikh temple). The consensus is that Sikhs should not eat meat because doing so would harm another living being. Once they become Amritdhari (baptized), they are forbidden from eating ritually-slaughtered meat because it transgresses one of the four restrictions in the Sikh Code of Conduct or *Rehat Maryada*.

Taoism: Tao or Dao is a Chinese word signifying "way", "path", "route" or "road". Tao, like Buddhism, is a philosophy, not a religion, and offers a general understanding of the Universe on which many Far Eastern religions are based. Tao is the natural order and primal power of the Universe that forges all phenomena and is eternally nameless. The Tao does not mention specific foods in most cases, so there is no reference to meat or dairy. Instead, it focuses on the nature of Miranda in the food.

According to the *Tao of Health, Sex and Longevity* by Daniel P. Reid (1989), the overriding Taoist principle of balance between Yin and Yang is established by harmonizing the Four Energies and Five Flavors in foods.

In Ancient Chinese philosophy, Yin and Yang is a dualism concept. The Universe created itself out of the chaos of material energy, organized into Yin and Yang cycles, and formed into objects and karmic lives. Yin and Yang are the extremes at the end of the continuum. Yin is the receptive and Yang the active principle, seen in all forms of change and difference, such as the seasons (winter/summer), sexes (men/women), temperatures (hot versus cold), tastes (sweet versus sour), etc.

The Four Energies are hot, warm, cool and cold. They define the nature and intensity of energy released in the human system when food is digested. Hot and warm foods belong to Yang; cool and cold foods belong to Yin. The former stimulates and generates heat; the latter calms and cools the organs. Too much of one energy imbalances health.

The Five Flavors are sweet (earth), bitter (fire), sour (wood), pungent (metal) and salty (water). Sweet influences the pancreas/stomach, bitter moves to the heart/small intestine, sour has an affinity for the liver/gallbladder, pungent affects the lungs/large intestine and salty associates with the kidneys/ bladder. When determining the best diet for you, you first look at the eating system. A balance between the five is the key to a healthy diet, but your body/metabolism type is also important, so you must pay attention to what works and doesn't work for you. If you tend to run hot or eat too many hot foods, you need to balance those with cool foods, for example.

One Daoist philosophy is bigu, which means "avoiding grains". Bigu is a fasting method where you eliminate grains from the diet. The person survives on a small amount of highly nutritious superfoods, including foraged raw foods, medicinal herbs and minerals. Bigu is believed to slow the aging process, detoxify the body, clean the digestive system and balance the body's energy. Some interpret bigu as eating nothing.

Indigenous Practices

There are, and have been for over tens of thousands of years, indigenous spiritual and ritual traditions globally. I don't have expertise in any of them beyond my exposure and what I could find in books and websites. I went to undergraduate school at Miami University, a school named after the Myaamia tribe. Miami students have long been educated in the traditions and history of the tribe. The tribe is deeply involved with the university and has a physical presence on campus.

Some of my knowledge also comes from prior participation in a Sacred Fire group; its principles are based on Huichol traditions.

My knowledge about the Mayans comes from the depth of information they left behind.

For the sake of brevity, I will reference a few North and Central American traditions as examples of broader patterns, given that I know more about them than other traditions. The Mayans, Myaamia, Chippewa, Hopi, Apache, Huichol and thousands of other groups called these regions their lands.

The overall pattern I see is an intimate relationship with the land and a sense of community.

The Huichol, Mayans and Myaamias do not double as names for religions. Their beliefs and practices have long been passed down by word of mouth. Each group has a relationship to the Earth that namelessly evolves. Since this is a 3D book, I have to use name identifiers.

The Huichol: The Huichol (or Wixáritari) are an indigenous people of Mexico living in the Sierra Madre Occidental range in Nayarit, Jalisco, Zacatecas and Durango. They are best known as the Huichol, but they refer to themselves as Wixáritari in their native Huichol language. Their lives center around sacred rituals and traditions, everything from planting corn to embroidering clothes. It is all done in a sacred way.

The Huichol were once considered a nation of Shamans. A Shaman is a person with access to and influence on the world of good and evil spirits. Often, Shamans enter a trance state during a ritual as they practice divination and healing.

Tribal members are subsistence farmers, and like other indigenous people, eat from the land and from what they can grow. Their main crop is maize, but they also grow beans and squash. Some raise livestock for milk, but they also sell the cattle to raise money from the meat. When they eat meat, it is usually acquired through hunting.

As is common among indigenous peoples who eat meat, tribal members have ritual appreciation practices for hunting and preparing it, including asking the animal's permission to take its life and expressing gratitude when it says "yes". The practices help mitigate potential harm from meat consumption.

The Mayans: Historically, the Mayans are one of the best-remembered groups across time because of their size, architectural heritage and calendar. They surfaced into popular culture in 2012 when their calendar allegedly predicted the end of the world. It didn't predict the end of the world; it predicted the end of an era, the era we are discussing in this book.

The Mayans lived throughout southern Mexico, Guatemala, northern Belize and western Honduras. They used astronomy, calendrical systems and hieroglyphic writing to communicate and understand the cosmos. They had elaborate and highly decorated ceremonial architecture, temple-pyramids, palaces and observatories, all built without metal tools. They were skilled farmers, weavers and potters.

The Mayans believed that most people's souls spent their afterlives in the underworld, a place filled with evil Gods represented by jaguars (night symbols). Only those who died at childbirth or were sacrificed could escape it. They also believed every person had an animal companion who shared their soul and could transform into that companion.

Their food came from the land: corn, squash, pumpkin, dipper gourd, Chiapas tomatoes, sunflowers, Amaranthus, agave and Tithonian. Corn was significant and had deity status. The Mayans ate "some" meat. Archaeologists determined that the Mayans hunted deer, peccaries and tapirs. They likewise ate fish, turkeys, dogs and bird eggs.

The Mayans understood that plants and animals had spirit and used plant spirits for healing. Their diet consisted primarily of what they could collect and grow in their region.

The Myaamia (Miami): A displaced Native American tribe, the Myaamia were originally located across what we know today as Indiana, Illinois, Ohio, Wisconsin and Michigan. It was among the Nations exposed to early European contact, first through the Jesuit mission in the late 1600s, followed soon after by the French and British invasion and the struggle for control of the Great Lakes region. In those days, the Myaamia numbered tens of thousands of people.

The people drew their sustenance from the wetlands, prairies, woodlands, river bottomlands and plants and animals that lived in those places. During the long summers, villages grew miincipi (Miami corn) and other vegetables. They dried, processed and stored these agricultural products to last throughout the year. The men of the villages helped in minor ways with the farming, but spent most of their time hunting moohswa (White Tailed Deer), lenaswa (Bison), mihšiiwia (Eastern Elk) and the wide variety of smaller animals and birds that populated the Waapaahšiki Siipiiwi and the hunting grounds to the east and west. During the winter, larger villages broke into smaller hunting bands and moved into winter camps located on or near the hunting grounds. In the early spring, the women and children moved to the sugar maple groves to collect sap and process the liquid into maple sugar that they ate, stored and traded. Following the return of warmer weather, the Myaamia began their agricultural cycle by clearing and planting their fields.

These vital cycles of planting, harvesting, hunting, gathering and processing governed the lives of the Myaamia for generations. The rhythms of the cycles reflect an ecologically-based existence in an ancestral homeland they call Myaamionki (Place of the Miamis). For the Myaamia, their land and the ability to care for their needs were the foundation of communal life and the basis of their health.

After a review of the tribe's website, I was unable to identify a published tie between diet and spiritual beliefs. However, their reverence for the land, and their communal way of life, shows a tribe that sees a relationship between it all.

Chapter Three

Food Quality and Vibration

Overview

The health and quality of the plants you eat impact your vibrational energy. The good health of any living thing has a higher vibrational energy than poor health. You'll want to eat the plants with the highest vibrational energy possible, and this chapter helps you sort them out. I can't tell you which plants are personally best for you. Some people love peanuts; others die if they eat them. I love tomatoes, but others are allergic to them. My mother eats onions like she eats apples, but others cry at the sight. Instead, this chapter looks at the broader picture of plant vibration leaving you to make choices. Growing location and methods also affect vibrational quality, and discussions on these are included.

Topics in this chapter include conventionally grown, genetically modified, organically grown, farming using natural agriculture and wild-grown. I also discuss the benefits of raw versus cooked food. Each subsequent chapter section is a growing method creating a higher vibration.

Conventionally Grown and Genetically Modified

Genetically Modified crops are relatively new, but farmers have been using pesticides for over 4,500 years. The first known pesticide was an elemental sulfur dusting in Sumer. Sumer is the earliest known civilization in the historical region of southern Mesopotamia, which occupies most of present-day Iraq and Kuwait. Next, we leap to the 15th century CE when toxic chemicals came on the scene. Arsenic, mercury and lead were applied to crops to kill pests. Synthetic pesticides in the USA arrived by 1930 and became widespread after World War II. Today, most farmers depend heavily on synthetic pesticides to control insects in their crops.

The term "Conventionally Grown" (CG) is used most often to describe crops treated using pesticides and chemical herbicides. Growers apply them to kill and distract various nonhuman sentient beings and to accelerate plant maturity. According to the Environmental Protection Agency (2021), organophosphates, pyrethroids and carbamates are the most commonly used insecticides. In 2001, insecticides accounted for 12% of total pesticides applied to the surveyed crops. Corn and cotton account for the most significant shares of insecticide use in the USA.

EPA reevaluates each pesticide's safety every 15 years. It insists that small amounts of pesticides and herbicides cause no harm to humans, but it provides no data. At what level is consumption safe or unsafe? Perhaps eating one apple is safe, but what if you eat a meal with other foods treated with the same amount of chemicals? And what happens to your body as the chemicals accumulate inside you over time?

According to the National Pesticide Information Center (NPIC):

The body stores many pesticides in fat before they are removed from the body by the liver or kidneys. Pesticides stored in fat can build up in larger quantities as we age. Because of this, older adults may experience health problems from pesticide exposures that may not cause problems for younger adults. The body also stores pesticides in the blood and other body fluids. Such pesticides may stay in older adults' bodies longer if aging kidneys are not as effective in removing them.

(NPIC, Online, Internet, 12/28/2021)

NPIC provides references for its determinations.

Any CG plant will have pesticides and herbicides inside and out. Many food preparers believe that washing the fruit or vegetables removes the chemicals. Some corporations sell produce washes for this purpose. I counted over 25 different brands on Amazon (I stopped at that number). Some of those brands used chemicals to remove chemicals, leaving a new residue. The FDA recommends washing fruits and vegetables in cold, drinkable water. Water rinses off residue or chemicals on the outside of fruits and vegetables. Using fruit/vegetable washes or dish soaps may result in the residue left on the produce and can also change the flavor.

Exterior washing of the plants before eating them won't remove all of the toxins. Plant skin is porous: What reaches the outside gets inside and can't be washed away. Also, remember that the plant grew up with pesticides and herbicides in its food: applied toxins were in the soil and thus absorbed into the plant.

Now to Genetically Modified Organisms (GMO). Genetic engineering is used to engineer a plant to enable a higher yield and distract pests. Engineering manipulates an organism's genes directly, e.g., transplanting DNA from other organisms. Sometimes, animal DNA is used creating a hybrid plant-animal. There is no consensus among scientists, yet, on whether or not GMO foods have any longtime risk for humans. The process is still too new. Until they decide, the crops are approved for human and animal consumption.

GMO foods have been on the USA market since 1994, ever since the introduction of Flavr Savr tomatoes engineered to ripen slower. Genetic engineering is a tool used for a variety of purposes. Most corn and soy grown in the USA have been genetically modified to resist herbicides. Other crops have been modified to withstand pests.

Genetic modification is not grafting, something we learned in high school botany. Grafting is a technique in which the tissue from one plant, the scion, is attached to another, the rootstock. The rootstock produces new vascular tissue to feed the scion, and the graft heals. Grafting, which resembles how plants combine their species without human intervention, is a natural way of combining two types of plant genetics and creating a third. With grafting, plants choose to integrate. GMO plants do not have that choice.

Some foods are more likely to be GMO foods than others. Here are some of the most engineered from a 2018 list: alfalfa, canola, corn, papaya, potato (mostly white), soy, sugar beet, zucchini and yellow squash. If you're unsure if a food is GMO before you buy it, and the package or sign doesn't tell you, you can assume that if it's a commonly-eaten food, it may be a GMO since that appears to be the trend. With declining acreage available for farming, and the need to grow more in a smaller space for an ever-increasing population, genetic engineering of the food is becoming increasingly popular.

The World Health Organization (WHO) reports that GMO foods "currently available on the international market have passed safety assessments and are not likely to present risks for human health. In addition, no effects on human health have been shown as a result of the consumption of such foods by the general population in the countries where they have been approved." (WHO, Online, Internet, 2021) The WHO is an agency of the United Nations responsible for international public health. It provides no scientific support for its claims.

The University of Connecticut (UConn) Agriculture College of Health and Natural Resources posted an article on GMO safety (28 December 2021). Diane Hirsch, Extension Educator, UConn Extension, the author, wrote, "Yet, science continues to suggest that there is no substantiated evidence that GMO foods are less safe than non-GMO derived food products. A 2016 report from the National Academies of Science, Genetically Engineered Crops: Experiences and Prospects, discusses human health. Claims regarding human health and safety of GMO foods included increased risks from cancers, kidney disease, obesity, celiac disease, diabetes and allergies. When comparing rates of these conditions in the USA, where GMOs are ubiquitous in the food supply to the UK, where essentially no GMOs are consumed, there were no significant differences." The authors did not provide data or references, so we can't judge the truth.

I also consulted WebMD, a good source for thoughtful medical opinions. Its opinion on the topic was equally blurred. They couldn't say yes or no, most likely because nobody yet knows.

Regarding spiritual nutrition, the point with GMOs isn't whether or not someone will get physically ill. It's about the genetic modification of plants using animal DNA. When you eat an apple, are you also eating a pig? If that's the case, you are eating animal energy. Does the plant's energy remain stable and high if animal energy is incorporated? Perhaps yes, perhaps no. Regardless, if I were you, I'd stick with plant-only energy to ensure you are getting the highest vibrational energy.

Agribusiness and Food Safety

Who decides whether foods are safe to eat in the USA? The decider is the USA Food and Drug Administration (FDA). The FDA is a federal agency of the Department of Health and Human Services responsible for protecting and promoting public health through controlling and supervising food safety, tobacco products and many other consumer products, including cosmetics. Its focus is the enforcement of the Federal Food, Drug, and Cosmetic Act (FD&C). The agency is led by the Commissioner of Food and Drugs, appointed by the President with the advice and consent of the Senate. The Commissioner, a political appointee, reports to the Secretary of Health and Human Services.

The FDA is a government agency led by a politician, making it subjectable to political winds. Anytime politics is involved in the conversation, I retain a safe amount of distance from what I hear. Because the FDA is politically led, I don't use it as a reliable source. I go directly to scientific research articles when I can find them. My intuition also steers me.

Agribusiness' political campaign donors are the second determiners of what's safe to eat, and politics is a money and power game. Often, when the FDA makes a safety decision, they consult juried science, which is the right thing to do. "Juried" means a nonpartisan peer review of scientists in the field free of outside influence. But the FDA is a political entity, meaning that they also "follow the money". "Follow the money" means that the influencer with the biggest check steers the FDA's decision.

Agribusiness funds research, conducts its own and contributes to politicians to ensure their profits grow. Below are the top ten agribusiness donors according to OpenSecrets (November 2021) in descending order of cash contributions. Corporations and individuals have other ways to contribute, such as networking, vacations, gifts, etc. Those contributions are off the official record. OpenSecrets acquired the data through publicly available sources (e.g., tax returns). I'm not trying to be a conspiracy theorist here, but you should be aware of money's influence. If you spend time in the political or corporate worlds, I'm guessing you aren't surprised.

Mountaire Corp is the fourth-largest chicken producer in the USA, and Grimmway is a carrot producer. Some of the companies have organic divisions, but organic farming isn't the primary business model. The list includes a few adjacent industries, including distributors, farm insurance and farm machinery.

1. Mountaire Corporation, $2,979,300
2. Grimmway Enterprises, $1,150,000

3. American Crystal Sugar, $681,410
4. McKee Foods, $472,989
5. Altria Group, $328,556
6. Deere & Company, $273,867
7. National Cotton Council, $261,035
8. Reyes Holdings, $247,835
9. International Paper, $223,022
10. Florida Crystals, $222,100

Organic

Organic farming is a crop production method that doesn't use (or minimally uses) pesticides, fertilizers, genetically modified organisms, antibiotics and growth hormones during cultivation. Some growers use the organic process for environmental and profit reasons and others entirely for profit, given that there is a demand. Organically grown food has a higher vibration than CG food because the cultivation process is closer to the natural process.

When we see the organic label in the store, what does that mean? Most people probably assume the plants were naturally grown without pesticides. They might also assume that the growers used the old ways of crop rotation, manure fertilization, etc. According to *Scientific American*, when the Soil Association, an organic accreditation body in the UK, asked consumers why they buy organic food, 95% said their top reason was to avoid pesticides. Many believe that organic farming involves no pesticide use, but it isn't true. Most organic foods are indeed grown and processed without "synthetic" fertilizers or "chemical" pesticides, but we can't assume the plants were grown naturally or pesticide-free.

The USA Federal government allows loopholes. Organic farming can use pesticides and fungicides to prevent critters from destroying their crops, just less of it. The top two organic fungicides, copper and sulfur, are used. Biopesticides are also used.

Biopesticides are made of living things, pose fewer risks than conventional chemicals and small quantities can be sufficient. They tend to break down faster, which means less pollution, but they aren't "natural". The USA Environmental Protection Agency (EPA) website (2016) defined biopesticides as follows: "Biopesticides are certain types of pesticides derived from such natural materials as animals, plants, bacteria, and certain minerals. For example, canola oil and baking soda have pesticidal applications and are considered biopesticides."

Not all those above-mentioned ingredients are natural. Canola oil isn't natural; it's made in a processing facility by slightly heating and then crushing the seed. Almost all commercial canola oil is extracted using hexane solvent, and recovered at the end of processing. Hexane is an alkane of six carbon atoms, with the chemical formula C_6H_{14}. Exposure to excess hexane can induce neurological symptoms.

Baking soda isn't natural, either. It's made from soda ash, also known as sodium carbonate. Soda ash is manufactured in two ways:

- by passing carbon dioxide and ammonia through a concentrated sodium chloride solution (table salt)
- mined in the form of an ore called trona

Regardless of organic farming shortcomings, the produce is better for you than CG and possibly GMOs. Organically grown food has a higher vibration, so I recommend buying it versus the other two options.

Natural Agriculture

Natural Agriculture (natural farming) is an ecological approach utilizing a closed system limiting human intervention. No fertilizers, herbicides, or pesticides are used. If insects or animals eat the plants, so be it. If there isn't enough water to grow the plants, so be it. The plant grows as close to nature's intent as possible. The "agriculture" part includes minimal farming with human intervention such as light weeding and adding a pole supporter. No fertilizers, compost piles or manures added to the soil. There may or may not be some weeding, but it's done by hand or with small tools. Some staking is also possible. Seeds are planted in prepared areas, "prepared" meaning that the farmer may lightly plow the ground to help the seeds take hold. The seeds are exclusively natural or organic.

The farmer also makes use of companion planting. Plants of different species grow together, helping each other, using the inherent communal nature of each other as a tool. One example of companion planting is a vine climbing a tree trunk to get more sun or vegetables planted next to each other to help each other thrive. One vegetable attracts pollinators, and another repels pests. One provides nutrients or shade for another. Marigolds are a good companion plant because they repel nematodes and other garden pests. Basil and tomatoes go together; the herb helps tomatoes produce greater yields and repel flies and mosquitoes.

Plants grown using Natural Agriculture are almost as spirit-filled as wild plants. The "help" the plants provide each other enters you when you eat, adding communal energy and thoughts to the ones you currently hold.

Wild Grown

Wild-grown food has the highest vibrational energy of any growing category, and the harvesting process is called "foraging". Living with wild-grown food is the most holistic way to eat: the food grows naturally and collecting it puts you in a relationship with nature. Wild-grown food is 100% the way nature intended to feed you. It is richer in essential vitamins and minerals, and foraging for it gives you much-needed exercise.

You can't eat the entire field or forest, however. Not every plant is healthy for you. Some of them are even dangerous.

For example, you wouldn't want to eat Poison Ivy or Poison Oak. To learn how to eat from the wild, I took a few classes from Pascal Baudar, the author of *The Wildcrafting Brewer*, and *The New Wildcrafted Cuisine*. We foraged and then prepared what we found along with wild foods he'd prepared in advance. He also brought cooking aids: a sun-heated oven for root vegetables and a propane burner for boiling. Earlier, he'd prepared the nut cheeses, salad, crackers, plant meatballs and other treats.

During the class, I learned to see the natural world differently. I began noticing every plant because we were looking for specific things to harvest, which made us examine everything. I was amazed at the plant diversity. I had no idea that so many different kinds of plants could exist in a square foot of space. He also pointed out the companion plants and how they helped each other.

I took a second class on beer making, crafting beer from what we found in the wild. I was surprised that you could make beer from almost anything, which was why the beverage has been around for thousands of years. Anybody with enough patience—and a desire for liquor—can make it. It requires a plant, sugar, water and fermentation time. I thought sugar came from sugar cane, but there is sugar in the wild; it grows from insect deposits on partnership trees and looks like white growths. I tried some. It was very sweet.

In the olden days, before the growth of cities, you could go into the wild and get wild plant food without thinking. That isn't true anymore. Today, foraging takes planning and thought unless you have a few acres in the country. Certainly, you can forage on your property and find things to eat—fruit from the trees, dandelions from the yard, flowers from landscaping. Today, however, you should be cautious of pollution. If you fertilize the lawn, don't eat those dandelions; they'll have pollutants in them, for example. If you live on a heavily traveled city street, auto pollution will contaminate front yard plants, so avoid those.

Consider these five things to do before foraging in urban areas:

1. Avoid toxic areas: Do not forage near busy roads or city-maintained parks. Most plants absorb lead and other heavy metals from vehicle exhaust. If you live in an area where it snows, cities may also use chemicals to clean the roads. Those chemicals seep into the soil near the road, and rain spreads the contamination. Also, keep in mind that some urban parks are sprayed with pesticides. What kills one living creature can damage another, and you are a creature.

2. Know what part of the plant is safe. The leaves may be edible but not the bark.

3. Know the water source. Eating plants grown in contaminated water means that the plants are contaminated. Causes for contamination include chemical runoff in farming areas, industrial pollution and proximity to streets and highways.

4. Be sure the plant is healthy before you pick it. When I took the foraging classes, the instructor showed us the difference between a wild wheat plant that was okay to eat and another with dangerous fungi.

5. Be sure you have permission to forage. Understand the city's laws about picking things on public property. Cities often have laws against picking plants from city parks, and I've heard stories of people who foraged in the park and got tickets from police or rangers. If you forage on someone else's property, ask permission.

Wild food has the highest vibrational energy and has the most information to share. If you can eat from the wild, do it. If you're not used to foraging, take a class or read about it. It's worth eating wild plants for the high vibration.

Raw versus Cooked

In addition to the debates on plant cultivation, many argue whether to eat plants raw or cooked. On a sliding scale, raw, wild food always has the highest vibrational energy and the most information, but either cooked or raw is fine. Not everyone's body is designed for eating 100% raw plant food in this incarnation, so follow your design.

One of the best-known authorities on eating raw plants is Dr. Gabriel Cousens, MD, ND, DD. He's a medical doctor, Rabbi, scientist, and an Essenian Priest; many of his books are listed in the Resources section of this book. His work is well-researched, thorough, and voluminous.

Cousens examined the nutritional value of raw food and advocated for its superiority to cooked food in terms of physical and spiritual health. I'll steer away from the physical, nutritional piece; it isn't this book's focus. If you're interested, you can read his work. Instead, I'll concentrate on the unmeasurable vibrational energy, which he calls "spirit".

His arguments for eating raw plants in his book, *Conscious Eating* (1992), made so much sense to me that I began eating 80% raw almost immediately. Eighty percent is his minimum suggested amount to get the full vibrational benefit.

I'll borrow an example from his research on Type 2 diabetes patients. Diabetes is the number one cause of adult-onset blindness, surgical amputations and kidney failure, three diseases stemming from a lower vibrational energy.

After three weeks of an 80% raw plant-based diet—a level considered "High Raw", most of his subjects lowered their blood sugars below the dangerous level. I tried this for myself, and it worked. At the time, my blood sugar level had recently reached the diabetes II danger zone. I did a nine-day fast and then ate 80% raw. My blood sugar level lowered, and I was no longer diabetic. So, for many of us, it works. You may automatically raise your vibration while curing (and/or preventing) the disease.

Cousens calls raw plant foods "restorative live foods". His arguments focus on the minerals within the food as "frequencies of consciousness, frequencies of light and frequencies of information", the driving forces of spiritual life. He believes that as much as 30% of our energy comes from the spiritual dimension, raw vegan foods are the best foods for nourishing that aspect.

His book, *Spiritual Nutrition*, discusses how raw foods maximize your gene expression. "If you eat live foods with lots of phytonutrients, you're going to turn on the anti-aging gene. You're going to turn on the anti-inflammatory genes. You're going to turn on the anti-cancer genes. And, if you eat junk food, you're going to turn those off." He adds that activating the growth hormone creates "youthing", turning back the clock to a biologically younger physique.

He adds, "that when eating raw, you'll eat half as much food. In addition to eating wholesome foods and ditching the Doritos, one of the keys to anti-aging is to drastically cut down on the number of calories you eat. In a recent experiment, rats that had their daily calories cut 40% had a whopping 400% increase in their anti-aging genes. That's a pretty important statement because it means we can reverse the aging process." Says Cousens, "Not that we can slow it down, that's true, but we can literally reverse it at any age."

After eating this way for a couple of months, my meditation practice deepened, colors seemed brighter, I heard more of what the plants around me had to say, and I felt cleaner and lighter inside.

I subsequently read all of Cousens' books and looked for more sources. I next found Janette Murray-Wakelin's book *Raw Can Cure Cancer*. I didn't have cancer, but I assumed that whatever was in her book addressed the benefits of raw food eating. She was given six months to live when Janette Murray-Wakelin was diagnosed with highly aggressive carcinoma breast cancer over six years ago. The tumor was 3 cm, and the cancer had spread into the chest wall and the lymph nodes. It was recommended that she undergo conventional chemotherapy and radiation treatment, which may possibly extend her life a further six months.

It was 2001. She was 52 years old, a mother of two and grandmother of one; she was not willing to accept this prognosis. After considerable research on natural ways to restore health, she built a fully raw diet that cured the cancer. The choice set her and her husband on an intentional journey to optimal health. As veteran ultra-endurance runners, they demonstrate that a raw, vegan-conscious lifestyle results in optimal health where anything is achievable physically, mentally, and emotionally.

A healthy body helps raise your vibration.

I wanted to learn even more, and I stumbled across Dr. Ann Wigmore's Natural Health Institute. The Institute is located in Puerto Rico by the ocean. Wigmore founded the school as an early pioneer in the use of wheatgrass juice and living foods. The school's staff is dedicated to teaching the purest form of the living foods lifestyle. The Institute is a place to reconnect body, mind, and spirit while rebuilding and rejuvenating. It prepares and serves only natural, raw plants.

I watched a cooking demo on YouTube offered by one of the Institute's chefs, Kaelash Neels. When I saw him, I assumed he was around 27 years old, and I was pleased with how much wisdom and skill he had for someone his age. I watched the video and then researched him. He wasn't 27; he was 43, which explained the skill and wisdom. He certainly didn't look 43.

Others on raw diets also looked amazingly young to me regardless of their age, and they seemed to have lots of energy. John Kohler of "Okraw" was one, and the list goes on and on. I figured that there was something to this raw plant diet. I was healthy, but the vibrant natures of the people I saw made me want that, too. I subsequently went fully raw for a 90-day trial, doing it for the nutrients and spirit connection. I saw the plants as sources of information and links to Earth, and the Hollywood Farmers Market became my friend.

I eat 70 to 80% raw because certain plant foods I find comforting. Still, that percentage is high enough, especially when mixed with my other spiritual practices (meditation, yoga, energy work, gratitude, etc.).

Chapter Four

The Coagulators

Overview

Water makes things flow, but coagulators make things jam—energy, blood, fluids, air. Coagulators include processed foods, salt, fats, and even excess protein. Think of them as dams in your body. You want fluids and energy to move freely because physical diseases and spiritual disharmonies emerge inside those dams. They also emerge when the fluids and energies can't reach where they're needed. Our physical body has systems to get rid of things and move stuff along, such as the urinary tract system, bowel movements, sweat glands, lungs and the breath, and a beating heart. If blockages inhibit their functions, disease and problems follow. Physical illness includes heart attacks, cancers, intestinal problems, congestion, organ malfunctions, etc. Spiritual blockages distort intuition, Source disconnection and can contribute to depression and anxiety. By Source, I mean the depository of energetic information from spirit guides and others. Blockages can also inhibit karmic growth and create negative energies spreadable to others. In other words, your energy-induced diseases are contagious.

It's hard to know when you have blockages until it's too late. They're slow to develop, and everyone's body does it differently. Most people won't have a heart attack after eating their first Double Whopper with onion rings, but if they eat them every day for a few months, all bets are off.

To illustrate this, I recommend watching the documentary *Super Size Me* (2004) directed and starring Morgan Spurlock, an American independent filmmaker. The film follows 30 days from 1 February to 2 March 2003, during which Spurlock ate only McDonald's food. The film documents the drastic effect this had on his physical and psychological health and well-being. His insides became "blockage central."

He ate at McDonald's restaurants thrice daily, trying every item on the chain's menu except salads. He consumed an average of 5,000 calories per day when an intake of about 2,200 could be considered the healthy limit. Consequently, the then-32-year-old Spurlock gained 24 lbs, his body mass increased 13%, and his cholesterol climbed to 230 mg/dl. He developed mood swings, sexual dysfunction, and fat accumulated in his liver. After his experiment had concluded, it took 14 months to lose all the weight gained by using a vegan diet supervised by his then-girlfriend, a chef specializing in gourmet dishes.

Yes, that was an extreme case, but it's a good example of how a diet high in saturated animal fat, processed foods, and salt affects the body. I'm sure that 5,000 calories per day of spinach wouldn't have had those effects. That's a lot of spinach, and he may have turned green in the process, but spinach has no blockage properties so it wouldn't have had those effects.

How will you know if there is too much coagulation? Medical testing can show you, but if you start having Spurlock-type symptoms, you're getting there. Once there, it can take a long time to return to good health. It took Spurlock 30 days to get sick and 14 months to get healthy.

Here's a story from another angle: How my clean internal body and energy system helped me. I was in Patagonia, Arizona, for a conference with Gabriel Cousens (mentioned earlier). In residence was Dr. Cromack, a chiropractor and energy practitioner, a professional offering his services to conference participants. At the time, I had a slightly humped back that perplexed me. The problem probably arose from previous negative self-concept issues as a youth and young adult, causing me to hunch over to hide myself.

According to Dr. Cromack, and the yogis who tell us the same thing, a curved spine limits energy flow. It can also lead to physical problems such as back and neck pain, and a fused spine. In later years, my head could lean forward. He said my back was curable, and we got to work.

He examined my back and neck muscles, joints, and bone structures. When he finished, I sat up, and he gave me some good news.

"You have 85% mobility in your neck. That's good for your age. I'll work on that, too, to give you a little more."

"Great," I said. "Thanks."

With a serious face, he said, "Before we start on treatments, I wanted to give you a heads-up. You're going to feel some discomfort while I'm doing this. If it's too much, let me know."

I cringed. "Discomfort" was a socially polite word for, "This is going to hurt," I assumed. I imagined being cracked and twisted in ways that wouldn't let me get up from the table. I told myself, "Stop imagining the worse. You'll be fine." I hate pain. I fear pain, but I trusted him. He was my age, for starters, meaning that wisdom and experience were among his tools. He'd also been sensitive enough to say something in advance. Not all medical practitioners offer warnings.

"Okay," I said, using my most confident voice. I laid on my back, closed my eyes, and eased into yogic breathing. I felt a strap go around the back of my head, and then he yanked. The yank was uncomfortable and sudden, but it didn't hurt. He tugged again a little harder, and I was still okay. He yanked a third time.

I felt a sudden dull pain and heard a crack in my neck.

He stopped. "Heard that?"

"Yes," I said. However, I felt no pain, which made me wonder if he was doing it the right way. I'd assumed the pain would be a sign of progress.

"I didn't break it," he said. "It broke up what was in the way and making it stiff. Are you okay?"

"Yes," I said. Still no pain.

"That's it for the neck. Can you roll over onto your stomach, and I'll work on your back?"

Whew, I thought. That didn't hurt at all. I rolled over.

He massaged my spine and ran a wooden tool over it several times. I felt pressure, the kind that makes you hold your breath for a few seconds until you realize you can breathe. It didn't hurt, however. The pressure application and hands-on massaging went on for about 20 minutes.

"All done," he said. "You can get up at your own speed."

I didn't feel any pain, but I got up slowly, afraid that any sudden move would put me into traction. It didn't happen, however, and I felt fine. I was amazed.

"You may feel some soreness tonight," he said, "but it'll be temporary."

Perhaps the pain would come later, I figured, like in the middle of the night. I said, "Thank you," regardless, working to sound nonchalant.

We scheduled a second appointment for the next day. That night, I felt no pain or stiffness, much to my relief. But there was another day of treatments, so maybe I'd feel pain from those.

When I came into his office, he asked, "How are you feeling?"

"Great," I said with a cool shrug. "No pain or discomfort."

"Yes," he said. "I find that plant-based eaters who avoid processed foods feel little-to-no pain and heal more quickly. That's probably why you're okay. Your bodies are cleaner. There's much less blocking your insides to create the pain."

End of story. What a relief, and what motion that was to keep it up. Next, I'll discuss all of those coagulators that could cause that pain if you consume them. I'll conclude the chapter with one of many solutions.

Salt

You're thinking, "Salt? I can't eat that, too?" Not exactly. Nobody can live without salt, so "yes", you need to eat some salt. The problem isn't salt. The problem is the quantity. Too much salt—a desiccant—holds onto stuff, especially moisture, as evidenced by those little desiccant packets inside electronics packages, prescription containers, and vitamin bottles.

Salt, a hygroscopic material, is an absorbent. It has an affinity for moisture, which is why we store it in sealed containers. When we put too much into our bodies, it ends up in the bloodstream. If more salt is in the stream than our body needs, the extra pulls water into the vessels, increasing the circulatory system's blood volume. With more blood flowing in the vessels, the pressure increases. Vessels are not infinitely large or elastic, especially if they're pressured over long periods. Even a balloon can handle only so much air before it pops. Vessels are alive and can tire; when they do, they say, "I've had enough," and break. Over time, high blood pressure may overstretch or injure the blood vessel walls and speed up the buildup of gunky plaque that can block blood flow. The added pressure tires out the heart by forcing it to work harder to pump blood through the body. Your kidneys and brain stress out, also. This can lead to heart attacks, strokes, dementia, and kidney disease.

Excess salt also holds onto water all over your body, too, causing you to gain weight. Extra weight creates a whole host of physical, social, and emotional problems. I've seen many people eat modest calories and low fat without lowering their salt intake. They don't lose weight, and some even gain. It's all about the water the salt clutches onto in the body.

"But the body needs salt," you say. Well, you're right. The problems are quantity and kind. According to the USA Food and Drug Administration (FDA), Americans eat, on average, about 3,400 mg of sodium per day. However, the Dietary Guidelines for Americans recommends that adults limit sodium intake to 1,500 to 2,300 mg daily. The latter is equal to about one teaspoon of table salt. Other organizations suggest that full-grown adults can get away with far less. According to the American Heart Association (AHA), the minimum physiological requirement for sodium is less than 500 mg daily—or less than the amount in one-quarter of one teaspoon of table salt.

Keep in mind that all packaged foods have salt in them. Even raw meat has added salt, which is listed on the package. There is also salt in every natural plant food. The salt of the earth becomes the salt of the plant. So, by the time you add the salt from the meat, the salt from dairy (especially cheese), the salt from the packaged foods, the salt you add to your cooking, and the natural salt with the plants, your daily intake of salt is far too much.

I do not eat meat or processed foods, and I don't add salt when cooking. I've learned how to prepare tasty foods without added salt. My daily intake is about 700 mg, which I get entirely from plants. That's within a healthy range, and it's doable.

"But it doesn't taste salty without added salt," you say? That's because you've been eating excess salt most of your life without knowing it, and that's what your tongue craves. You've eaten what your family and friends ate. You've lived on packaged food from the grocery store and fast food from the restaurant. Your taste buds adjusted long ago. But guess what? It's been too much salt the entire time. If you're afraid to live with less of it, you may have an addiction to it.

I experienced this after a nine-day fast at TrueNorth Health Center, where I went for a fasting cleanse. I did not eat food for six days, consuming only water, and then TrueNorth gradually reintroduced food the last three days. Day one was juice only. Day two included "some" solid plant foods (unprocessed). Day three was more food. All the food was 100% plants with no added salt, oil or sugar.

On my last day, I created a fresh salad at the food bar that included tomatoes. I love tomatoes. After the first bite, I needed a glass of water because the vegetables—especially the tomatoes—were too salty. Before that, the salad would have probably needed some salt. After the fast, I no longer needed it and realized that I'd been over-salting my diet.

For salt substitutes, I use vinegar, lemons, limes and spice blends. Celery is a salty vegetable. My homemade vegetable broth includes a lot of celery.

Processed Foods

Was it processed in a plant or did it come from a plant? If it's the former, avoid it. If it's the latter, include it. This is an important ascension-related question because processed foods lower your vibration given their artificial ingredients. Some of the chemicals within them don't leave your body without much extra help, too. If they stick around, they can reduce your vibration over the long term.

Processed foods are created in a food factory. When they're made and packaged, they almost always include plenty of salt, oil, sugar, dyes, and preservatives. The end-product needs these because they serve as preservatives and addictive agents. The closer to fresh it is, the quicker it'll spoil and decompose. You want to eat as close to the earth as possible. Processed foods take you in the opposite direction.

When I was 11 years old, I got my first chemistry set, and it came with a warning: "Do not touch or consume the chemicals." It was clear that they weren't made for human consumption, or at least not in those amounts. If my body took them inside, I'd get sick.

Processed food includes chemicals from the chemistry set, albeit in allegedly safer doses. According to the USA Federal Drug and Administration, which tests foods before they reach the market, small amounts of chemical additives are harmless.

The Feds are probably correct for a single serving, except that's not how most Americans eat. They don't sit down with a plate with a single serving once a day. Their plates (meaning the meals and snacks) consist of many different foods over the day, and if a lot of them are processed, they're consuming considerably more chemicals than those few in a single serving.

I had my first bodily-awakening of this after applying the principles in the book *The Whole30* by Melissa Hartwig Urban and Dallas Hartwig (2015). I'm not recommending the book because it presented a case within a carnivore diet, but it made a good point about processed foods. I was intrigued by a discussion about chemical accumulation in the body. The authors posited that bad things for us stick around in our bodies just like good things, and they similarly impact our health. The "30" part of the plan included the suggestion to eliminate chemical-enhanced foods for 30 days and watch what happened to your body. I tried that, and I noticed a difference. I'd lost ten pounds, felt lighter, and had more energy by the end. That was enough proof for me.

I did additional reading elsewhere and learned about bioaccumulation. It's a scientific term describing the gradual accumulation of substances, such as pesticides or other chemicals, in an organism. It occurs when "an organism absorbs a substance at a rate faster than that at which the substance is lost by catabolism and excretion". The longer the biological half-life of a toxic substance, the greater the risk of chronic poisoning, even if the toxin's environmental levels are not very high.

According to Ana Sandoiu in *Medical News Today*, in an article titled "More evidence that ultra-processed foods could harm health" (May 2019), Cancer, Type 2 Diabetes, Celiac Disease, and Multiple Sclerosis are just a few of the outcomes associated with consuming processed foods. Some studies have also suggested that consuming processed meat may raise the risk of premature death.

This is one of many articles on the topic. If you want a real-life story, I recommend reading *When the Music Stopped: My Battle and Victory Against MS*, by Bob Cafaro (2015). Bob is a cellist with the Philadelphia Orchestra. In early 1999, he was diagnosed with Multiple Sclerosis (MS). MS is a disease in which the immune system eats away at the protective covering of nerves. With MS, resulting nerve damage disrupts communication between the brain and the body. As a cellist in one of the top five orchestras in the country, the disease posed career and health risks.

The book details his battle against the disease and how he won. At the time, there was no medical cure, and he described his hopelessness and the many things he tried to fight the disease. Eventually, he turned to a mix of an unprocessed vegetarian diet, an improved mindset, and an exercise regimen, all of which proved successful. His mix might only work for some. Everyone needs to find their mix. But he made the point that health can be restored with a combination of a healthy mind, body and spirit.

Our bodies know how to get rid of bad things, but not at the quantities they encounter. Our immune and defense systems can handle trace amounts of the bad stuff, but that's it. When too much "bad" gets in, our systems fall apart, our vibration lowers, and we sink into ourselves.

Many Americans unknowingly eat several processed foods per day, and I will illustrate the impact by taking you through a single meal common for many and a weekend treat for some: a burger, fries, and soda. Americans eat many of these meals at least weekly, as evidenced by the burger franchises nationwide. Most restaurants serving "American food" have this meal combination. In Los Angeles, 267 franchise locations specialize in burgers. That doesn't include the 30,000 diners and the mom-and-pop restaurants too numerous to count. Within three blocks of my apartment, there's a Rally's, a Fatburger, a Habit Burger, a Wendy's, a Carl's Jr., an In-N-Out, a Jack in the

Box, and a diner. Two McDonald's restaurants are five blocks away in either direction.

All of these meals involve some kind of additive. Some advocate them as "natural" because they are promoted as "plant extracts". Here are a few: pyrrolizidine alkaloids, glycoalkaloids, glucosinolates, glycosides, saponins and psolarens. But what does "extract" mean. When we think of the word, we assume that someone stuck a needle into an apple and withdrew the juice, but that isn't how it works. Sure, the extracting process pulls something out of the plant, but then "the something" gets processed and given a name we can't pronounce because it is no longer natural. Fructose corn syrup is a plant extraction combination, but few argue that it's good for you. Anything natural is served in its "whole" state.

Below, I itemize the burger and fry meal and list each item's additives and information sources. The amount of each additive is small, but they add up. Some of the sources I list are outside the USA given that the food industry is international. You could be eating things at a Cleveland McDonald's that came from China, where the standards are different than in the USA.

- *Ground beef:* Acetic acid, alginates, ascorbic acid, carrageenan, citric acid, locust bean gum, guar gum, potassium acetate, sodium acetate (National Institutes of Health)
- *Bun:* Corn dextrose, corn maltodextrin, dough conditioners (monoglycerides, DATEM, ascorbic acid, enzymes), vinegar (McDonald's website)
- *Ketchup:* Malic acid, potassium chloride, sucrose (Heinz website, *Irish Times*)
- *Mustard:* Xanthan gum (Heinz website)
- *Pickle slices:* Calcium chloride, potassium sorbate, potassium aluminum sulphate, polysorbate 80 (McDonald's website)

- *Tomato slice:* Cyprodinil and/or boscalid methamidophos, methomyl, difenoconazole (National Institutes of Health)
- *Onion:* Cypermethrin, chlorpyrifos, difenoconazol, or/and λ-cyhalothrin (National Institutes of Health)
- *Lettuce:* Cypermethrin, chlorpyrifos, difenoconazol, or/and λ-cyhalothrin (National Institutes of Health)
- *French fries:* Cypermethrin, chlorpyrifos, difenoconazol, or/and λ-cyhalothrin (National Institutes of Health)
- *Diet Coke:* Aspartame, acesulfame K, caramel E150d, phosphoric acid, sodium citrate (Coca-Cola)

In just one meal, you had four (not one) servings of cypermethrin and cyprodinil, two insect repellents. When you read the package, the list of chemical additives is often longer than the food. There are often unlisted chemicals, such as anything used to make and grind the white flour. The sources listed above as "Heinz" were websites reporting what Heinz had told them. The food labels didn't list these additives.

The lesson here is if you want a healthy body and an ascension-ready vibration, stick with pure whole foods.

Fat

Another coagulator is fat: animal fat, plant fat, dairy fat, nuts and seeds and avocados. If you want to observe how fat works, wash your dishes after an omnivore meal, especially if you fried bacon, broiled a steak or baked a chicken. Washing the dishes takes a lot of soap and hot water to clean off that fat. You can also watch how the fat dilutes the soap. And then there's the fat inside the oven and on the kitchen's walls. It's everywhere. The same is true when you use oils, even if you don't cook with them.

Once fat sticks to a surface, it doesn't want to come off, whether inside your body or out. It clings to the walls of your arteries and elsewhere, holds onto new fat from subsequent meals, and thickens your blood. This "hold" blocks vibrational flow. Blocked vibrational flow lowers your energy frequency. It becomes a sponge for toxins, thoughts, and feelings by slowing down your body's ability to flush them out, creating pockets of poison within you, especially if you don't get enough water and fiber.

You're probably surprised that the list includes plant fats, especially if you eat a raw vegan diet. Many raw vegans rely on fatty foods such as nuts, seeds, avocados and coconut as diet staples. But fat is fat, albeit plant fat is better than animal fat. You can get too much plant fat, too. Your body needs "some" fat to operate, but most plants have fat, which adds up like salt. Even broccoli has fat.

One of the best sources of scientific opinion and research on the coagulative effects of fat is the work of Dr. Caldwell Esselstyn, Jr. Esselstyn is a physician and researcher at the Cleveland Clinic in Cleveland, OH. It's a worldwide multispecialty academic medical center integrating clinical and hospital care with research and education. Dr. Esselstyn received his BA from Yale University and his MD from Western Reserve University (now Case Western Reserve University). His scientific publications number over 150, and he's listed in the 1994-95 edition of *The Best Doctors in America*.

In 1995, Dr. Esselstyn published his benchmark long-term nutritional research on arresting and reversing coronary artery disease in severely ill patients by putting them on a plant-based diet free of fat. That same study was updated 12 years later and reviewed in his book, *Prevent and Reverse Heart Disease*. In July 2014, he reported the experience of 198 participants seriously ill with cardiovascular disease. During 3.7 years of follow-up of the 89% adherent to the program, 99.4% avoided further major cardiac events.

Dr. Esselstyn's research was one of the longest longitudinal studies of its kind, and he's not alone in his findings. Dr. Michael Greger reported similar results in his analyses, and Western medical doctors are catching up. Greger is a researcher, medical doctor, and author of *How Not to Die*, and they aren't new findings. My father, who died in 2008 from heart disease, got similar advice in the 1980s (advice he didn't consistently follow).

How much fat is safe? Dr. Esselstyn says zero added fat given that there is fat in most plant foods. All scientists say you need "some" fat, and they are right, but it's easy to get it from plants that we think are fat-free. There are .3 grams of fat in an apple, for example, and 1.8 grams in a cup of cooked brown rice. Fruitarians are healthy without eating nuts and seeds. They get all the fat they need from the fruit. You can reach your full daily fat requirement without adding a single walnut. I do it. I'm editing this page at 2:19 p.m., and so far, I've eaten 10.9 grams of fat, according to Cronometer.com. The principal sources have been quinoa (boiled in water), chia seeds (for the Omega 3), pomegranate seeds, and bananas. I'm at 7.9 grams so far. My maximum is 12 grams for the day, and I'll land there without eating nuts, seeds, avocados or oils.

So, where's the line on fat? It depends on who you ask. According to Anthony William in his book *Cleanse to Heal*, a food is considered fatty—or "Radically Fat"—if the calorie intake consists of 51% or more of fat. A literature review on athlete health and fat indicates that fat should stay between 10% to 15% of daily calories.

Healthline.com presents a comprehensive table summarizing what many understand. Runners should consume the least amount of fat because they need to stay lean and have a fast-moving inner system. Ten to 12 grams is recommended for them. Football players eat a higher level of given their need to be heavier. The suggested range for football players is 20 to 25 grams. The average life expectancy of a jogger is 84 years. The average life expectancy or lifespan of an American football NFL player is 53 to 59 years depending on playing position. *The Washington Post* reported in 2015 that the average American consumes 65% of their calories in fat, which is 44 to 77 grams per day. That's way too much. If you want to stay lean and healthy, I suggest keeping your fat intake closer to the average runner than the average American.

If ten to 15 grams is healthy, why do so many Western medical doctors recommend between 20 to 25? The answer is simple: The average American is already eating twice that amount or more, and suggesting that they drop to ten to 15 is unrealistic, so they offer a compromise.

There is no mutual agreement in the literature about how much fat is too much or enough, and there probably won't be an agreement any time soon. Bodily systems are diverse and therefore tough to uniformly categorize. Doctor knowledge about fat levels vary, especially in this world of specialties where no one doctor knows everything. Doctors are just as susceptible to marketers and lobbyists as anyone else. The meat lobby is powerful.

How much is right for you? Listen to your body and intuition. As long as you don't fall below ten grams per day on average, you're fine.

Protein

Protein consumption falls into the "Oh really. I can't eat that either" category. The answer is, "Of course you can, but—" Protein consumption (types and quantities) is one of the most controversial subjects. I could buy the Empire State Building if I collected a dollar every time I heard the question, "How do you get your protein?" I even get the question when I eat out. When I go to Chipotle for a salad, and we approach the meat section, I'm often asked, "Which protein do you want?" My response?

"There's enough protein in the beans and brown rice. I'm good. Thanks." That response generates a most puzzled look on the worker's face. The look is no surprise because the worker is inundated with the "meat is protein" mantra by the media, coaches, and athletic trainers.

The next question is, "How much?" The oft-quoted personal training world posits 120 grams per day to build muscle, but that's way too high. The medical community recommends half that amount. I build muscle with 45 grams.

"There's a misconception that because we all eat, understanding nutrition is simple," said Valter Longo, director of the Longevity Institute at the University of Southern California. "But the question is not whether a certain diet allows you to do well for three days, but can it help you survive to be 100?"

In a 2013-14 study, Longo's research team followed over 6,300 adults over the age of 50 to see what effect high, medium, and low protein diets had on longevity. The authors said that people in the study ate 16% protein, two-thirds coming from animal sources, a typical American diet. A high-protein diet was defined as 20% of one's daily calories coming from protein. A moderate-protein diet had 10-19% calories from protein, and a low-protein diet consisted of less than 10% protein.

According to the study, people aged 50-65 who ate high-protein diets were four times more likely to die of cancer, which is the range of smoking risk, said the authors, compared to people who ate low-protein diets. Moderate-protein dieters were three times as likely to die from cancer. People who ate high-protein diets were 75% more likely to die from any cause, including three times as likely to die from diabetes. The team calculated that reducing protein intake from moderate to low reduced the risk of death by 21%.

Yes, protein is a builder. It builds by filling in the cracks and surrounding your cells with tight wraps. But excess protein can be suffocating. It's like dressing your young daughter to go out into 35-degree weather wearing a thick onesie coat, a scarf wrapped around her neck, a woolen hat on her head, mittens on her hands, and then adding layers until she's the shape of a pickling cucumber. The child can't move or breathe. Problems erupt.

Why are the public recommendations for protein consumption routinely high? One of the best explanations for the conventional protein push comes from Dr. Greger of NutritionFacts.org. The nonprofit organization conducts meta-analyses of scientific research on health and nutrition. A meta-analysis is a statistical analysis combining the results of multiple scientific studies. Meta-analyses can be performed when multiple scientific studies address the same question, with each study reporting measurements that are expected to have some degree of error.

In his analysis, Dr. Greger provided a thorough overview of the history of the protein push in an 11 April 2019 article titled "Changing Protein Requirements". I summarize and paraphrase the findings below.

According to Dr. Greger, the incorrect protein recommendations we live with were created a century ago. These recommendations were later reinforced in the 1930s when a disease of malnutrition called Kwashiorkor was introduced. The disease was named and defined by Dr. Cicely Williams, a Jamaican researcher. Kwashiorkor was assumed to be caused by protein deficiency. The finding took flight and became a part of the protein mantra and our excuse for eating lots of meat.

It turns out that her original proposition, which led people to want more meat, was based on an untested theory. Once the theory was tested, scientists learned that "there is no real evidence of dietary protein deficiency" as a condition for the disease. In other words, the laboratory testing results didn't back her up. The scientists learned changes in gut flora were the likely causal factor for the disease, not protein deficiency.

Of course, like anything else, the first significant piece of news hitting the press and airways is what people remember, even though the facts do not later support the story. While realizing her mistake, Dr. Williams spent the latter part of her life trying to debunk the reason for the condition she had described but to no avail. Through today, most think we need a lot of protein, and that meat is the source.

By the 1970s, science had accumulated a body of research that destroyed the theory of pandemic protein malnutrition. Infant protein requirements went from a recommended 13% of daily calories down to ten percent, seven percent, and then five percent.

How much protein do we need? According to the laboratory studies researched by Gregor's team, "Adults require no more than 0.8 or 0.9 grams of protein per healthy kilogram of body weight per day, which is about your ideal weight in pounds multiplied by four and then divided by ten. So, someone whose ideal weight is 100 pounds may require up to 40 grams of protein a day. On average, they probably only need about 30 daily grams of protein, which is 0.66 grams per kilogram, but we round it up to 0.8 or 0.9 grams because everyone's body is different. We want to capture as many in that suggestion as possible."

Gregor continued. "People are actually more likely to suffer from protein excess than protein deficiency. The adverse effects associated with long-term high protein/high meat intake diets may include disorders of bone and calcium balance, disorders of kidney function, increased cancer risk, disorders of the liver, and worsening of coronary artery disease. Considering all of these potential disease risks, there is currently no reasonable scientific basis to recommend protein consumption above the current recommended daily allowance."

To track your daily consumption, you can use an online food diary like Cronometer.com. I do that from time to time. Today at noon, I've reached 24.7 grams from the following sources:

- Quinoa, 5.5 g
- White beans, 5.3 g
- Raw oat cookie, 3.5 g
- Raw spinach, 2.6 g
- Coconut water, 1.8 g
- Pomegranate seeds, 1.2 g
- Chia seeds, 1.1 g
- Raw carrots, 0.5 g
- Raw pineapple, .5 g

Excess protein can create disease, and disease lowers vibrational frequency. Not enough protein can do the same. Plant sources provide more than enough. The best sources are nuts, seeds, beans, tofu, nut butters, quinoa, and brown rice. If you eat a healthy balanced diet, you should get all you need without thinking.

Psychic Attacks

Disclaimer: A psychic attack is an energy food, not a 3D traditional food. Regardless, it's a food that that lowers your energy. I'm not including this category to alarm you but to create awareness. The result of a psychic attack (negative energy flying at you) is energy coagulation, which is covered in this chapter.

On this planet, negativity is going to come at you no matter what. It happens to all 3D and 4D energies. You may even be the thrower. Attacks could be as simple as a moment of frustration or as harsh as a knife in the back. The point here is to help you prevent an attack, recognize it, and have the tools to deal with it.

What Is a Psychic Attack? A psychic attack is an invasion of our energy and life force. It drains you, blocks the flow of positivity, and causes emotional or physical harm. It's a lower vibrational energy assault on your energy field.

An attack happens when an energy entity or human being intentionally or unintentionally sends negative energy your way. The attack could be as simple as thinking negatively about you or wishing you'd become ill. If the attack is unintentional, it usually comes from people who don't know how to process their emotions when they feel hurt, so they wish a world of hurt on the person who hurt them in return. It's why I say throughout this book to focus on positive thoughts towards yourself and others. You could be unintentionally attacking both your energy and the energy of others.

You can receive a psychic attack from anyone: friends, family, coworkers, strangers, and disembodied souls. A disembodied soul is the continued coalescence of a person's energy once it leaves the deceased's body. It sticks around either because it doesn't believe it's dead or because it has a protection or retribution agenda.

The negative energies are usually projected as anger, jealousy, envy, or other emotions. The inflicted harm on you can affect your emotional, physical, spiritual or mental state. It is understood that when negative energy is consciously sent to someone to inflict harm, it returns to that entity whether or not it harms you. It's the universal law of karma.

Why Attacks? There are three categories of psychic attackers: incarnated souls, disincarnated souls, and Negative Polarity (NP) entities. Each has a different reason for their attacks, so I'll break them into groups for discussion.

Incarnated Souls: An incarnated soul lives within a human body. You, the reader, are an incarnated soul. Here are some of the most common reasons for an attack from an incarnated soul.

- Jealousy: The victim's life progresses while the attacker's is stagnant.
- Envy: The attacker is envious of the victim's looks, career, life partner or environment.
- Negative emotions: The attacker is living on their dark side at the moment.
- Fear: The attacker lacks self-conviction and is living in fear.
- Energy theft: The attacker, an energy vampire, takes your higher vibrational energy to lift its own.

Disincarnated Souls: A disincarnated soul was the soul inside a human body until the body died. The soul hangs around either because they don't know they're dead or because they have an agenda. Here are some of the most common reasons for attack by a disincarnated soul.

- They want to pay back someone who hurt them or someone they loved.
- They want to ensure that their final wishes are honored.
- The attacker wants to protect what a person loved or what it built during the incarnation, such as a spouse, business, estate or a body of creative work.

I experienced this kind of attack after my father died. He was a good person and built a good business, but he and I didn't see eye-to-eye over many things, which created tension between us. I eventually learned to block his attacks while he was alive, but I wasn't prepared to block them after his death. They only lasted a month after his death, but here was the most salient attack.

After he died, I came home to Cleveland from New York for a week to comfort my mother and help plan the next steps. After a day, I took on cleaning up his home office and organizing it. My father had been reasonably organized throughout his life but was less organized later. I made a few discoveries that I won't get into here. None of them were illegal, but they showed his less-organized side in the later years.

He evidently wasn't happy with what I discovered and revealed, which resulted in a broken finger. Since then, I've learned self-protection techniques, but unfortunately, I was without them.

One evening, my mother asked me to go into the basement and retrieve something from the freezer. I had an eerie sense of doom when I walked down there, so I quickly grabbed the package and moved to get out of there. At the base of the stairwell, my left arm involuntarily rose quickly and slammed against the wall, cracking a bone in the middle finger of my left hand. I immediately sensed my father's presence. Unfortunately, this was before I learned self-protection.

Negative Polarity (NP) Entities: As mentioned earlier, NPs are energy beings from other dimensions who want to keep the Earth's energy at 3D. This group of attackers comes from other planets and dimensions and wants to keep the Earth at a lower vibration. NPs tend to target higher vibrational humans such as Lightworkers and psychics. Most of the psychic attacks I receive are from NPs, and I have tools for prevention and cleansing.

How Do You Know? We all feel icky from time to time because of physical illness, sensitivity level or psychic attacks. How do we know the difference? Your intuition is the best source of recognition, but I discuss nine more below. Keep in mind that you should couple your intuition with each of these to learn the reason behind them. Sometimes, the reasons are karmic and not attacks. I knew my father's soul was the attacker because the energy of the basement warned me and I felt my father's presence. Just now, I spilled an iced coffee onto the floor at a coffee shop. My intuition said, "You've had enough. Drinking anymore of this isn't good for you." The episode resulted from a spirit guide coming to my aid, not an NP attack.

Bad Luck: You may experience a streak of bad luck. The episodes can be subtle things that come out of nowhere, like spilling coffee, locking your car keys in the car, or losing your wallet. They can also be extreme, like losing a job, being in a car accident, or breaking a leg. Experiencing a series of adverse events can signify a psychic attack.

I tend to have a lot of good luck, but things happen out of the blue, like losing my West Hollywood library card right before COVID hit; it was on my key chain one day and gone the next. I didn't get a message that it was done to protect or teach me, so I attributed it to a psychic attack. Without the card, I couldn't check out books virtually for pickup. I couldn't get a new card. There was nobody to speak with to get another card. It was a whole year before I finally spoke to a human and solved the problem. In the interim, I used the Los Angeles Public Library.

Blocked Creativity: You're usually creative—you write books, sing professionally, or engineer buildings. But suddenly, you can't do any of it for a prolonged period—longer than usual—and you're frustrated and worried. Has your creativity well dried up? Probably not. It's likely a creativity block, but it could also be a psychic attack, so listen to your guides. I faced this situation when writing this book. I started it in 2019, and it rolled along for about two months, but then I stopped. I couldn't do a thing; nothing came out of me. I tried and tried. To fix the problem, I hired an energy healer, got rid of the blocks, and voila—here's the book.

Brain Fog and Forgetfulness: Setting aside too much coffee, wine, or not enough sleep, an attack can cloud your brain and impair your thinking, especially if you're a clear thinker with a good memory. I'm seldom forgetful and a relatively clear thinker. I also set up many crutches just in case: Google Calendar, spreadsheets, and phone alarms. When Smart Phones became available, I was relieved to have such a ready organizing device in my pocket.

Brain fog is another issue. Brain fog is a cognitive issue that can inhibit concentration, create dizziness and confusion, and interfere with your inability to recall everyday words. Here, I'm talking about temporary brain fog. It could be a neurological issue worth investigating if you have regular, long-term brain fog.

Depression, Negative Emotions, and Suicidal Thoughts: You needn't worry about acute depression. Most people have them. Sometimes, the moments are due to a past life memory flash, and other times to an episode that would make most people sad. This happens to me. I am sensitive to worldwide emotions and sometimes react to them as if they're happening to me. I recognize what's happening and have some tools to deal with them. They seldom persist for more than an hour.

If your depression persists, it could be due to several reasons, including a psychic attack.

Check with your guides on the cause and what you could do to come out of it. Sometimes depression manifests from physical, dietary, and traumatic episodes. You may have to consult a 3D professional such as a medical doctor or counselor.

Doubt: Doubt is on a continuum from "frozen in place and can't move" to momentary. Both can be due to psychic attacks. The former may require intervention from a professional, but the latter is something resolvable by your self-empowerment with help from your guides.

A slap in the face from a psychic attack can knock you out even if you're usually the most confident and forward-moving person on Earth. A friend of mine experienced an episode of this that built into immobilization. Eventually, he pulled out, but he was stuck in neutral for a few months.

He was fired from a job because of his age. He was 66 years old with a clear head, and considerable skill, and was liked by employees and clients. He was doing a fantastic job, but his peer-age supervisor was replaced with a much younger person who was intimidated by him, and she fired him without any reason. His separation agreement highlighted the passage that said he would sue for age discrimination. Nothing else was highlighted. Except for a comment made by his supervisor about his age, he had no evidence of age discrimination he could present in a court of law.

He was in shock and spun in place for months, filled with doubt. Was he a failed professional? Would his age block him from moving on? He got some help from a Lightworker who did energy work on him, ridding him of negativity and severing the tie between him and his attacker. He came back slowly, hiring a consultant to help and moving forward. Today, he is fully employed again and loving his job.

His firing was a psychic attack.

Fatigue: Assuming you don't have a physical illness, constantly feeling tired and depleted of energy for no reason could signify an attack. You eat healthily. You had plenty of sleep. You're in a good mood and then wham: You're exhausted. The exhaustion could be an energy vampire taking energy from you. We've all been there. I'm sure you have your own stories.

What is an energy vampire? Vampires could be friends, family members, or coworkers who zap your emotional energy. Energy vampires tend to prey on highly sensitive, empathic, and happy people and feed off their kindness and compassion until they leave them drained of their energy.

Negative Thoughts: You're doing well, having a good day, and then out of nowhere, you experience a sudden flood of dark thoughts. This can happen when negative vibrations are sent your way. It's fleeting, but there they are. When that happens to me, I stop and ask my guides where the thought emerged. Once I know—or even if I don't know—I sever my cord with the attacker and I deliberately think positive thoughts or find something pretty to focus on.

Nightmares: I recently listened to a video by Brian Scott, author and YouTuber of *The Reality Revolution*, about psychic attacks. He included this as a symptom with a story about his own experience that turned on an intuitive memory.

To create a healthier vibration, we must relieve ourselves of past anchors. I'd long assumed that the nightmares were emotional clearings brought about by help from my guides. According to Scott, that might not be the case. It could be a psychic attack, and you want to guard against them. You may still have nightmares, but they will be emotional clearings versus psychic attacks. I provide some preventive methods below, but I also discuss Scott's ritual in Chapter Seven.

Sudden Headaches: When we experience a psychic attack, our energy, soul, and body feel it. Tension and pressure in the area where the Third Eye Chakra and Crown Chakra are located (forehead and top of the head locations) are common signs to watch. Chakras are energy centers in the body, and those two have the highest vibrational rates making them ready targets. The pressure may manifest itself in a short or long-term headache. I am seldom attacked this way, but when I am, the headaches are quick announcements but aren't painful. I'm grateful for the warning, however. Warnings trigger me to stop and block the energy. If yours are prolonged and painful, I suggest a two-pronged approach: visit your medical doctor and undergo an energy cleanse.

What Can You Do About Attacks? Your options are prevention and post-attack clearing. I'll begin with prevention because that's always the better option. I suggest doing these three things daily if you can. The goal is to cleanse yourself of attacks in residency, and block or cleanse new episodes.

1. *Diet:* All sentient beings experience psychic attacks, so you don't want to eat something with attacks in their DNA, which means animals. You'll experience enough attacks without incorporating more of them through your diet. Plants aren't sentient, so you don't have to worry about them.

2. *Chapter Seven Solutions:* I offer several preventive solutions in Chapter Seven, including forgiveness, gratitude, mana force, meditation, mindfulness, story revision, positivity, and usefulness.

3. *Smudging:* Smudging, or other rites involving the burning of sacred herbs or resins. Smudging is a *way to energetically cleanse a space to invite positive energy.* Sage is the herb most recommend, and is readily available in metaphysical stores and grocery stores such as Whole Foods. Sage helps cleanse negativity and promotes healing, wisdom and longevity. During a smudge plant leaves or stems are placed in the container and ignited (preferably with

a wooden match). The flames are then gently blown out and the smoke, which heals the mind, heart and body, is wafted over the person, either by hand or with an eagle feather.

If an attack happens, here are six tools for post-attack clearing.

1. *Identify the attack and the attacker.* Attacks are often announced by sudden changes in thought, mood, or physical feeling. You can also identify them through the symptoms listed above. If you can't identify the attacker, don't worry. Just realize there is one, and that is enough.
2. *Check your fear.* Fear is gasoline for the attack. Don't be afraid; it's just an energy thing. It isn't real. It's stoppable.
3. *Ask your Higher Power for the source.* If you don't recognize the source or the message is unclear, simply imagine an energy field as the attacker. A Higher Power is a guardian angel-type extension of yourself available for protection and guidance.
4. *If you know the attacker personally, approach* her/him/them (if you can) and resolve the conflict between the two of you. If the attack was intentional or from someone who insists on holding on to their negative thoughts, then stay far away from the person.
5. *Cut the cord* between you and the source and tell him/her/them/it to leave you alone. If you can't identify the source, cut the cord to the ghost energy, asking for help from your Higher Self if needed.
6. *Engage professional help* if the above five activities don't work, I suggest you find a true Lightworker to clear your chakras and/or receive clean energy infusion.

Here is an example of how prevention helps mitigate nightmare attacks. This nightmare stems from a lifelong worry of whether

I've fulfilled all of my responsibilities, especially as a college student. I used to have these nightmares frequently, and they never resolved well. I was always negligent with my duties, waking in a sweat with my heart racing. I'd received professional help from a Lightworker long ago and had gotten rid of these nightmares, but then one came back and included a twist.

Before bed, I'd gone through all of the "before I go to bed" protections but still had a short series of negative energy dreams just before I awoke. One involved a school project that was due which I'd completed, but I was stopped from submitting it by a glass parking garage door that closed in front of my car as I tried to enter. I sat in the car and called the professor from my cellphone. He didn't believe me about the problem, but I negotiated with him and turned in the project. Whew!

I asked my Spirit Guides for the attacker's identity, but I didn't get a response. So, I imagined the energy being, cut the cord between us, and asked the being to leave me alone. That was the end of it all, including future dreams on this theme.

What About Calcium?

Calcium doesn't coagulate inside you, but you can get too much or too little. Either way, physical problems can erupt, and the problems can lower your vibration, much like a coagulant. Too much calcium can lead to a condition called Hypercalcemia. According to the Mayo Clinic's website, too much calcium in your blood can weaken your bones, create kidney stones, and interfere with how your heart and brain work. The Mayo Clinic is a nonprofit American academic medical center focused on integrated health care, education, and research in Rochester, MN.

The Clinic suggests a Recommended Dietary Allowance (RDA) of calcium for adults, varying by gender and age. By gender, the clinic means physical gender. I do not know how it work for transgender individuals. They would have to check with their physician.

The following bullets provide a guide for calcium level. Please note that the first column refers to "Physical Gender".

- Men 19-50 years, 1,000 mg/day, upper limit 2,500 mg/day
- Men 51-70 years, 1,000 mg/day, upper limit 2,000 mg/day
- Men 71+ years, 1,200 mg/day, upper limit 2,000 mg/day
- Women 19-50 years, 1,000 mg/day, upper limit 2,500 mg/day
- Women 51+ years, 1,200 mg/day, upper limit 2,000 mg/day

As a vegan, I frequently hear, "But where do you get your calcium if you're not consuming dairy?" There are plenty of plant sources for calcium. According to the Cleveland Clinic, the top sources include broccoli, dried peas, beans, kale, collard and dark green leafy vegetables. WebMD, a respected health-promoting website, also mentions figs, soybeans (tofu, tempeh), bok choy, oranges, seeds and winged beans. These aren't the only sources, just the sources with the most. There are plenty of plant sources of calcium for plant-based eaters. The added perk to these sources is that they come with little fat.

Chapter Five

The Anticoagulators

Overview

In the previous chapter, I outlined things that coagulate in your system and block energy flow. Fortunately, other things—the antidotes—can keep your systems humming and your energy flowing. Keep in mind that if you're eating poorly, engaging in negativity, or exposing yourself to toxins, you won't be able to solve all of your problems with antidotes. This is not a category of "pill practices" to keep you going when you're harming yourself. Yet the antidotes will help. And, if you're eating a vegan diet with fat, oil, sugar, and processed foods, it'll automatically improve your flow and health.

I discuss four additional "natural" antidotes, given that natural practices lift your vibration: consuming fiber and water and engaging in movement activities such as yoga and exercise.

Fiber

Dietary fiber, or roughage or bulk, includes the parts of plants your body can't digest or absorb. Unlike other food components, such as fats, proteins, or carbohydrates—which your body breaks down and absorbs—it doesn't digest most of the fiber. Instead, fiber passes through your stomach relatively intact, then the small intestine, and colon. This makes fiber important for carrying waste through and out of your body, the stuff you don't want hanging around inside. It's a continual spring cleaner. "Waste" is the digested part of what you eat that the body no longer needs. If waste sticks around too long, it poisons your system, making you ill.

There are two kinds of fiber: soluble and insoluble. Soluble fiber dissolves in water to form a gummy gel. It can slow down the passage of food from the stomach to the intestine. Examples include dried beans, oats, barley, bananas, potatoes, and soft parts of apples and pears. Insoluble fiber is often called "roughage" because it does not dissolve in water. It holds onto water, which helps produce softer, bulkier stools to help regulate bowel movements. Examples include whole bran, whole grain products, nuts, corn, carrots, grapes, berries, and peels of apples and pears. Animal foods have no fiber. Only plant foods have fiber.

The "dietary fiber hypothesis", first proposed in the 1970s, zeroed in on fiber as the dietary component protective against chronic disease. Dr. Greger, of NutritionFacts.org, reviewed the literature in May 2018 and determined that since the '70s hypothesis, the evidence accumulated to show that those who eat lots of fiber appear to be protected from several chronic conditions.

The Cleveland Clinic website posits five ways that fiber protects our health, and they're all about flow:

1. Lowers cholesterol: Soluble fiber has been shown to lower cholesterol by binding to bile (composed of cholesterol) and taking it out of the body. This may help reduce the risk of heart disease.
2. Better regulates blood sugar levels: A high-fiber meal slows down the digestion of food into the intestines, which may help to keep blood sugars from rising rapidly.
3. Weight control: A high-fiber diet may help keep you fuller longer, preventing overeating and hunger between meals.
4. May prevent intestinal cancer: Insoluble fiber increases the bulk and speed of food moving through the intestinal tract, which reduces the time for harmful substances to build up.

5. Constipation: Constipation can often be relieved by increasing the fiber or roughage in your diet. Fiber works to help regulate bowel movements by pulling water into the colon to produce softer, bulkier stools. This action helps to promote better regularity.

Holding onto waste makes your body ill, and illness lowers your vibration. Fiber is a cleansing tool keeping your body clean and your energy flowing smoothly.

Exercise

"It's better to eat junk foods and exercise a lot than to eat healthier and not exercise at all," wrote Dr. Paavo Airola in *Worldwide Secrets for Staying Young* (1982, p. 158). Exercise is important for digestion, bone and muscle maintenance and cleansing through sweat. You likely know that already. I think we all know it. But many of us struggle to follow through. Eating and watching television is far easier than getting up and moving, especially after a long day at work.

The vibration in raw plants is terrific for you, but it's not enough. Exercise gets your energy flowing. It helps you feel better, and positive feelings lead to higher vibrations. Exercise gets and keeps you healthy, and good health is also important for building your vibration. Exercise shakes up the Yang to wake up the Yin.

A study by Emma Childs and Harriet de Wit in *Frontiers in Physiology* (2014, 5:161) reported that physical activity had long been considered beneficial to health. Regular exercise relieves stress. The study compared psychophysiological responses to an acute psychosocial stressor among individuals who did or did not report regular physical exercise. Healthy men and women (N=111) participated in two experimental sessions, one with the Trier Social Stress Test and one with a non-stressful control task. They measured heart rate, blood pressure, cortisol, and self-reported mood before and at repeated times after the tasks. Individuals who reported physical exercise at least once per week exhibited a lower heart rate at rest than non-exercisers. A higher heart rate poses stress on the body.

In a study published in *Brain, Behavior and Immunity,* posted on the University of California San Diego Health's website, one 20-minute session of moderate exercise can stimulate the immune system, producing an anti-inflammatory cellular response. Just 20 minutes.

The Mayo Clinic weighs in, too. It recommends "regular" exercise and posits the following five health benefits based on research:

1. Exercise controls weight, and consistency is the key. The more intense the activity, the better.
2. Exercise combats health conditions and diseases. Being active boosts high-density lipoprotein (HDL) cholesterol, the "good" cholesterol, decreasing unhealthy triglycerides. This keeps your blood flowing smoothly, which reduces your risk of cardiovascular diseases.
3. Regular exercise helps prevent or manage many health problems and concerns, including stroke, metabolic syndrome, high blood pressure, Type 2 Diabetes, Depression, Anxiety, many types of Cancer, Arthritis and falls. It can also help improve cognitive function and lower the risk of death from all causes.
4. Exercise improves mood. Physical activity stimulates various brain chemicals that may leave you feeling happier, more relaxed and less anxious.
5. Exercise boosts energy. Regular physical activity can improve your muscle strength and boost your endurance by delivering oxygen and nutrients to your tissues and helping your cardiovascular system work more efficiently. And when your heart and lung health improve, you have more energy to tackle daily chores.

For healthy adults, the USA Department of Health and Human Services recommends that you get at least 150 minutes of moderate aerobic activity or 75 minutes of vigorous aerobic exercise a week or a combination of moderate and vigorous activity. One hundred fifty minutes equals 21 minutes per day. The guidelines suggest that you spread out the exercise during the week. At least 300 minutes per week is recommended to provide an even more significant health benefit and assist with weight loss or maintaining weight loss. But even small amounts of physical activity are helpful.

Strength training exercises for all major muscle groups are also recommended at least twice a week if you can. Aim to do a single set of each exercise using a heavy weight or resistance level to tire your muscles after about 12 to 15 repetitions.

You need Yin and Yang—the push and pull—to move from a 3D to a 5D world, a world of balanced Yin and Yang. From a vibrational energy perspective, exercise gets your Yang moving and engages your Yin to acquire balance. It's the battle your karma faces to resolve issues. The two don't balance independently. They have to work to find peace and equality, and exercise puts that into motion.

You can exercise anywhere: At the gym, at work (up and down the stairs) or outdoors. One hundred percent outdoors is ideal if you can do it. The outdoors puts you into automatic contact with live plants, nature spirits, and the water in the lakes, streams and oceans. The Sun's energy finds you outside, an excellent enriching source. It is more vital that you get the exercise than to wait until you can do it outdoors, however. I've long done a mix of inside and out:

- cycle and strength training at the gym
- parking at the far end of the parking lot instead of closer to the door
- walking outside during lunch

- using the stairs instead of the elevator
- making copies at the central copier versus the printer on my desk
- and urban hiking or cycling on days off

Whichever way you choose to get exercise, the goal should be to enjoy it. For some, it's walking. For others, it's running. Some enjoy tennis; others pickleball. Airports and train stations make accessible settings for strolls while you're waiting for departures. I have always enjoyed exercise, even when I was overweight. It makes me feel good, lifts my energy, and serves as a form of meditation.

Water

Fiber may act like a backpack for carrying waste to the door, but water is the lubricant. Water is also an essential energy conductor and an absorber of thoughts and emotions. Consequently, water significantly affects vibrational flow and is a central pillar of spiritual nutrition.

Most scientists believe that our body weight is 50 to 75% water. Blood is 90% water. Without water, we cannot maintain a healthy body temperature, lubricate joints, digest food, or eliminate waste. Insufficient water leads to dehydration, causing muscle weakness and cramping, a lack of coordination, and an increased risk of heat exhaustion and heatstroke. Most scientists believe that water is so vital to our body that we can't last more than five days without it.

The Purity Issue: One of the funny things about water is that we never think about it in its purest sense nor about the value it provides. We think about getting enough "liquid". We think of coffee, tea, milk, juice, alcohol and soda. We drink because we are thirsty or because we enjoy the taste and texture. Sometimes we drink for a pick-me-up or a slow-me-down. Social pressure sometimes leads to drinking. We often drink without thinking about the contents of what we're drinking and whether or not the ingredients are helpful. Indeed, water is a base for all beverages, but so many of those beverages have lots of additives, choking the water's original purity. If craft beer were essential to drink, the rivers would flow with it and the fish would swim in it. I guess the clouds would be brown, too, come to think of it.

Some of the liquids mentioned above aren't entirely bad for us. Juice has vitamins. Most teas are made from dried flowers or green leaves, which also contain vitamin power. But we also need pure water. Do you want coffee-infused blood or an alcohol-saturated liver? Probably not. The pure stuff makes what the system is designed to use to maintain health.

Pure water is also critical for retaining and managing prana. Water conducts energy and serves as an electrical (energy) transformer because it's made of crystals. Pure crystals are better conductors than polluted crystals. The crystals can be polluted by more than a tangible substance, however. Negative thoughts, words, and sounds can also pollute; they distort the shapes of the crystals, causing them to malfunction.

I first learned of negativity's impact on water crystals in the late 1990s while waiting for a train in the London Tube. I was in London doing doctoral dissertation research. I'd just entered the Lancaster Gate Tube stop to take the train to the National Portrait Gallery for a private showing of Nathan Field's portrait. I was working on Field's biography as a dissertation chapter. Field was a Shakespearean actor and playwright. While I waited for the train, I looked at the walls and saw posters of the photographic work of Dr. Masaru Emoto (published in 2004 in *The Hidden Messages in Water*). The photos introduced me to the impact of thoughts on our well-being.

Emoto's photographs showed how water connects deeply to our individual and collective consciousness. Drawing from his research as a scientist, he described water's ability to absorb, hold, and retransmit human feelings and emotions. Using high-speed photography, he found that crystals formed in frozen water reveal changes when specific, concentrated thoughts are directed toward them. Music, visual images, words written on paper and photographs also impacted the crystal structure. Emoto theorized that since water can receive a wide range of frequencies, it can also reflect the Universe. He found that water from clear springs and water exposed to loving words showed brilliant, intricate and colorful snowflake patterns, while polluted water and water exposed to negative thoughts formed incomplete, asymmetrical patterns with dull colors. Emoto posited that since people are mostly water, and the Earth is 70% water, we could heal our planet and ourselves by consciously expressing love and goodwill.

Each poster photo on the Tube's walls had a different image from Emoto's work. Printed at the bottom of each was the precondition of the crystal's formation—the negative or positive word, the negative or positive thought, etc. The difference between the positive and negative preconditions was clear: Positive stuff created clearer, brighter, and often more symmetrical crystals than negative.

Emoto also tested physically polluted water and found that cleaner water crystals were more symmetrical and healthier-looking (clearer, etc.) than polluted water crystals. Crystals would also be purer if we did not put pollutants into our bodies or the Earth. He showed us that physical and emotional influences could influence the physical quality of water.

That was the end of my negative talk, thinking or actions. No more watching films with violence. I spoke less. If I had a comment to improve something, I did it constructively and thoughtfully. I never again said, "You can't do this," or "You look so fat." The ten minutes in the London Tube changed everything.

Which Water to Choose? Now that you know how to keep the water pure, we move to finding ways to buy it that way. The purer it is before it goes into your body, the less time and effort you'll have to spend fixing it later (if it's fixable).

Several varieties of water are available, and I will discuss the most common types below: alkaline, mineral, purified, spring and tap. The definitions of each come from The International Bottled Water Association 2021 (IBWA), except tap water, which came from the Los Angeles Department of Water and Power.

Artesian water/artesian well water is water from a well that taps a confined aquifer (a water-bearing underground layer of rock or sand) in which the water level stands at some height above the top of the aquifer. Well water is water from a hole bored, drilled, or otherwise constructed in the ground, which taps the water aquifer. Mineral Water is natural water containing not less than 250 parts per million total dissolved solids. It is distinguished from other bottled water types by its constant level and relative proportions of mineral and trace elements from the source's point of emergence. No minerals are added to this product.

Purified water is produced by distillation, deionization, reverse osmosis or other suitable processes while meeting the definition of purified water in the US Pharmacopoeia. Other suitable product names for bottled water treated by one of the above methods include "distilled water" if it is produced by distillation, "deionized water" if it is produced by deionization, or "reverse osmosis water" if the process used is reverse osmosis. Reverse Osmosis is a technology that is used to remove a large majority of contaminants from water by pushing the water under pressure through a semi-permeable membrane (works like a filter).

Spring water must be collected only at the spring or through a borehole tapping the subterranean formation feeding the spring. Spring water collected using an external force must be from the same underground stratum as the spring, must have all the physical properties before treatment and must be of the same composition and quality as the water that flows naturally to Earth's surface.

Tap water comes from surface water (reservoirs, rivers and lakes) or groundwater (artesian and deep wells). Before it goes into the city pipes, it undergoes a disinfection process, destroying many harmful organisms like bacteria and parasites, albeit not all. It can only kill known bacteria and parasites.

In conclusion: Which water should you choose? From an energy perspective, any of them are fine. The water most natural from the Earth and pure are the best. Tap water is the worst because it can pick up bacteria, metals, and other things through piping. If you drink tap, I'd suggest buying a purifier for your home. It won't remove everything, but it'll help. I also recommend asking your guides and intuition for advice.

No matter which water you choose, thank it before drinking it, and ask the Angel of Disarmament to disarm its impurities.

How Much Water? "How much water should you drink?" According to Dr. F. Batmanghelidj in his book *Your Body's Many Cries for Water*, you take half your weight and multiply that by one ounce. If you weigh 160 pounds, you need 80 ounces of pure water (not juice, tea, soda). That's one opinion, and a common one at that, but you should also consult with your spirit guides and doctor. Everyone's body is different.

Yoga

Yoga is a spiritual development practice enabling the body and mind to self-observe and become aware of its nature through physical postures and movements (asanas). Yoga is also a way to live, eat, think and respond to the world. It's a way of being that results from the mindfulness you grow into as you do this spiritual practice. It's also a system enabling smoother energy flow within.

Many people shy away from yoga because they anticipate being forced into pretzel-shaped positions. They get this view from the pictures of skinny young women in tights twisting themselves into shapes inspired by Cirque du Soleil. I often hear, "Why do we have to contort our bodies into those shapes? I'm in no condition to tie myself into a knot." Well, that's not the kind of yoga I'm talking about here. Pretzel yoga is American gymnastics, however. It's based on the need to feed an ego, not develop energy flow or mindfulness. It isn't yoga any more than mustard isn't ketchup.

The kind of yoga I'm promoting is the original, energy-moving yoga. If you can sit in a chair, you can do it. A whole style of asanas for people with mobility issues is called "Chair Yoga", taught in nursing homes and senior centers. If you decide to take a chair-free yoga class, asana modifications are available if you can't do a pose, and the teacher will show them to you without judgment. You won't even have to ask. They'll notice you are struggling and offer to show you an alternative. Sometimes, the teacher will demonstrate alternatives as part of teaching an asana. I can't do a shoulder stand pose, for example, but there's a modification that works just as well for me.

To ensure you don't end up in a gymnastics yoga class, you'll need some background. The Yoga Alliance, a USA-based nonprofit membership trade and professional organization for yoga teachers, provides it for you. You should look for this type of yoga.

Yoga was developed up to 5,000 years ago in India as a comprehensive system for wellbeing on all levels: physical, mental, emotional and spiritual. Today, many millions of people use various aspects of yoga to help raise their quality of life in such diverse areas as fitness, stress relief, wellness, vitality, mental clarity, healing, peace of mind and spiritual growth. Yoga is a system, not of beliefs, but techniques and guidance for enriched living. Among Yoga's many source texts, the two best known are the *Yoga Sutras* and the *Bhagavad Gita*. Both explain the nature of—and obstacles to—higher awareness and fulfillment and provide a variety of methods for attaining those goals.

When I wanted to learn yoga, I looked for a school that met this definition. I was living in New York City at the time where I found Integral Yoga Institute of New York, a nonprofit organization dedicated to the practice and teachings of Integral Yoga, as taught by Sri Swami Satchidananda. The Integral approach integrates the mind, body and spirit, and intends to give students the tools to live peaceful, healthy, joyful and useful lives. It seeks to inspire students to find fulfillment in themselves and promote a peaceful existence with others. Integral was (and still is) both an ashram and a teaching center offering classes in yoga, meditation and spiritual development. It used to have a vegetarian grocery store and a boutique with natural body care products, albeit they are closed. Integral taught Hatha yoga, posited as the original style.

There are dozens of yoga styles in North America, of which Hatha is one. New styles emerge as students take yoga teacher training programs and assign their names to subsequent teaching practices. Many of their techniques are stretching and exercises versus energy-moving yogas. The intent of yoga is lost, so avoid those. I'm trained in two original practices: Hatha and Kundalini. Either is acceptable for you, but any style focusing on spiritual and energy development should be okay.

A class called "Hatha" usually means you'll get a gentle introduction to the most basic yoga postures. You won't work up a sweat (unless you sweat easily), but you'll leave the class feeling taller, looser and more relaxed. Hatha is an old system that includes asanas and pranayama (breathing exercises), which help bring peace to mind and body, preparing you for deeper spiritual practices such as meditation. Hatha is a generic term for yoga that teaches asanas intended to release and move energies within. According to the *Encyclopedia Britannica*, Hatha's origins are traced to Gorakhnath, the legendary 11th-century founder of the Kanphata Yogis, but it grew out of yogic traditions dating back at least as far as Patanjali (2nd century BCE or 5th century CE), author of the Hindu classics the *Yoga Sutras* and the *Mahabhasya*.

The practice of Kundalini yoga arouses the sleeping Kundalini Shakti (snake-like thing) from its coiled base through the six chakras that reside along the spine and through the seventh chakra, or crown. The style includes meditation, chanting, mudras and breathing exercises. Kundalini is known for its fluid, movement-intensive practices. The intention is to link the breath to movement. Kundalini yoga can be more physically demanding than Hatha, but alternative poses are available. Everyone can do it.

When choosing a yoga teacher, return to this chapter for the definition presented by Integral Yoga and compare the yoga teacher's intent to The Yoga Alliance or Integral's positions. You want the teacher to be within that frame or purpose. Also be sure to check the teacher's reviews on Yelp or other social media.

Chapter Six

Eating for Design

Overview

The reasons for raising your vibrational frequency are universal. How we get there is individual, and I'll explore some tools you can use to individualize your practice. Each of us differs, so one tool doesn't fit all. This chapter discusses body design, food coloring, and geographical eating to help you individualize your plan. These are the necessary spare parts hanging around the edges, an assortment of equally important things.

Body Design

Our bodies are crystal collections, and no two crystals are alike, which makes each person's body different from the others. Consequently, no single diet (or idea) can work for everyone or work similarly. It's safe to say that eating a lot of raw plants is suitable for most, but which plants should you eat? I'm equally sure that a diet of 100% Doritos isn't good for most, probably nobody. Yet the differences between what your body needs compared to mine are real. Many in the media and elsewhere insist that their single diet is the only and the best way to get to where you need to be, but they're selling a product or a reputation, so they have to lean reductionist or lose money and power. Truthfully, everyone needs to individualize their approach. But how do you know your approach, at least in terms of which foods could be better for you than others?

Trial and error and intuition are the best ways to determine which foods are better for your body. Not even "identical" twins are truly identical. An identical twin is a pair of beings having developed from a single fertilized ovum. They're alike because they begin with the same genetic characteristics (including sex) and are typically very similar in appearance.

Twins have the same genetic structure but begin with different personalities and experience life uniquely. Once out of the womb (and maybe inside of it), everything in their environment teaches, feeds and molds them. Their karmic souls will also differ: Just because they were born genetically equal doesn't mean everything is equal. They (we) are more than our bodies. Our bodies are merely vehicles in which the soul rides to learn. It's the soul that's in charge. Each twin begins the incarnation with a different set of purposes. If one of the incarnated twins is meant to be a medical doctor in this life and the other a Broadway musical dancer, their internal vibrational framework will differ. The vibrational difference reshapes each to fulfill their karmic lessons.

Once out of the womb, the twins live independent lives even though they may spend a lot of time together. If they're in the front yard playing, and a loud red car rolls by, one may look up while the other continues playing. That moment of different experiences shaped each of them uniquely. Throughout their lives, the changes made by the moment multiply and influence how they view things. Look at them like two glasses of water 25% full. Into one, you put a blueberry; into the other, some red paint. Then one gets a stone the size of a thumb, and the other gets a leaf. The things that go into each change the water's color, texture, etc. It's how life works for the twins as well.

You couldn't find four more different people than my parents' four children. None were twins, but we all came from the same genetic parents. One sister loved science and climbed trees. Another was shy and found her way into interior design. Another expressed herself physically through athletics and twirling a baton with the marching band. I was an emotional musician who hated sports. Same genetic founding, but four different people.

Years later, two of us (myself and a sister) underwent DNA testing as adults. I was amazed at the differences in the results. I'd assumed they'd be the same given, but significant differences appeared. I was 47% Northern European, mainly UK, Scandinavia, and Ashkenazi Jew. I was also 49% Mediterranean Rim with a chunk of Greek, 3% Middle Eastern, and 1% South Asian. My sister—same parents, same grandparents—was primarily Italian with smidgeons of Northern European. There wasn't one ounce of Jew or Middle Eastern in her.

Genes are essential, but the environment plays a big role. I'll return to the twin story and will create a fictitious pair of identical twins to illustrate. Every experience, no matter how small, impacts each twin differently. Ariel was born at 1:41 p.m. and Eyal at 1:42. Eyal came out excited, kicking his brother in the head. If you do astrological charts for each, even if they were born a minute apart, contrasts will foreshadow differences in personality, choices, and life directions. The differences might be slight, but "slight" is enough to propel them in different directions. It's like two cars going down Sunset Boulevard in Los Angeles. One driver holds steady on the wheel, heading straight down the middle of the lane. The other turns the wheel slightly to the left and will eventually change lanes.

Let's jump ahead to when the twins turn 4 years old. They've now had four years of life in similar contexts, yet not the same, further delineating their personalities and bodies. This morning, they're sitting in front of a television screen watching Blue's Clues while their dads are preparing a Saturday breakfast of oatmeal pancakes with honey-orange syrup. Ariel, who has a gift for music, opens his mouth to sing the theme song. Eyal likes to draw, so he takes crayons to paper.

The boys' eyes are glued to the screen. Ariel's head bobs to the beat as he sings. Eyal's eyes transfix on the house on the hill on the screen, and he chooses a crayon with an orange color to match the house. Each boy absorbs the cartoon differently because of who they have become to date. Their new experiences and perceptions from this program also create newly learned matrices that differ based on their internal designs. Those matrices absorb and change based on the unique experiences, making the two boys even more diverse than before watching the show. The effect is cumulative. The more experiences the boys have over their lifetimes—different or similar—the more the matrices will shape them independently.

How do you know what foods and experiences are right for you? There are three ways to learn. First, listen and pay attention to your body, which is my system. Are you allergic to nuts? Don't eat them. Do tomatoes give you skin issues? Don't eat them. Does eating fat raise your cholesterol? Don't eat it. Are you drawn to certain plants, and they nourish you? Eat them.

A second way to know is to listen to your spirit and intuition, another one of my tools. If you're sitting in front of a bowl of ice cream and something inside screams to leave it alone, dump the ice cream in the sink or give it to someone else. If you're at the farmer's market and an organic apple falls to your feet, it's for you. If a little kind voice in your head says, "Eat more greens," eat them.

A third way to know is to follow a spiritual dietary system based on body type. I'm not a fan of body types nor an expert, but they've helped guide people for thousands of years, so they are worth mentioning. They are handy if you're new to tapping spirit guides and your intuition. Body type systems are a good place to start.

What is a body type? A body type is the basic structure of your body's needs nutritionally and at a soul level. The best way to know is to follow intuition, but many theorists present body structures to guide you. The most commonly discussed are Ayurveda (Indian), Eight Constitutional (Korean), and male/female energy.

Ayurveda addresses the energy versus the physical body and looks at the balance between male and female energy. When discussing these energies, they have nothing to do with gender. You could be genetically and physically male but have predominantly female energy. We'll get into this in more detail later, but female energy tends to be the softer, more inclusive and intuitive energy. Masculine energy tends to be bolder, stronger, and a builder. Most of us are a combination of both energies, so it's important to know how to identify and feed the balance. Each body type system is designed to give you a healthy body and a smooth internal energy flow.

Ayurveda: The Ayurvedic Diet provides guidelines for when to eat and what to eat. It also offers ways to eat to boost your health, prevent or manage disease and maintain wellness. By following an Ayurvedic diet, you will eat primarily whole or minimally processed foods and practice mindful eating rituals.

According to the Ayurvedic Institute, a school teaching traditional Ayurvedic Medicine and Indian therapies, scholars consider Ayurveda the oldest healing science. Ayurvedic knowledge originated in India more than 5,000 years ago and is often called the "Mother of All Healing". It stemmed from the ancient Vedic culture and was taught by accomplished masters to their disciples in an oral tradition for thousands of years. In Sanskrit, Ayurveda means "The Science of Life". The principles of many of the natural healing systems now familiar in the West have their roots in Ayurveda, including Homeopathy and Polarity Therapy.

Ayurveda helps to comprehend and maximize the relationship between your physical body and its energy. It identifies three basic types of energy present in everyone, grouped into roughly three doshas (categories) to help us understand: Vata, Pitta and Kapha.

- Vata is the energy of movement.
- Pitta is the energy of digestion or metabolism.
- Kapha is the energy of lubrication and structure.

The cause of disease in Ayurveda is a lack of proper cellular function due to an excess or deficiency of Vata, Pitta or Kapha. All people have the qualities of Vata, Pitta and Kapha, but one dosha is usually primary, one secondary, and the third least prominent. The presence of toxins can also cause disease.

In Ayurveda, body, mind, and consciousness work together to maintain balance. They're understood as different facets of your spirit-physical being. Learning how to balance the body, mind and consciousness requires understanding how Vata, Pitta and Kapha work together. According to Ayurvedic philosophy, the entire cosmos interplays the five great elements' energies — space, air, fire, water and earth. Vata, Pitta and Kapha are combinations and permutations of these elements; they form the physical body.

According to the Institute, Vata is the subtle energy associated with movement and is composed of space and air. Vata governs breathing, blinking, muscle and tissue movement, pulsation of the heart and all movements in the cytoplasm and cell membranes. In balance, Vata promotes creativity and flexibility; it produces fear and anxiety out of balance.

Pitta expresses the body's metabolic system and is made of fire and water. It governs digestion, absorption, assimilation, nutrition, metabolism and body temperature. Pitta promotes understanding and intelligence; it arouses anger, hatred, and jealousy out of balance.

Kapha is the energy that forms the body's structure; it is made up of bones, muscles, tendons and provides the glue holding the cells together. Kapha is formed from earth and water, and supplies the water for all bodily parts and systems. It lubricates joints, moisturizes the skin and maintains immunity. In balance, Kapha is expressed as love, calmness and forgiveness; out of balance, it leads to attachment, greed and envy.

Do you want to know your mix of body type? The chart below will help, and you can estimate your own percentages. I created this "dosha chart" after viewing various sources, albeit I liked the format from *Ayurveda Healthy Living*. I'm about 60% Kapha, 25% Pitta, and 15% Vata.

1. Vata
   a. Elements and qualities: air and ether, dry, light, cold, rough, subtle, astringent
   b. Balance: perceptive, creative, artistic
   c. Mind imbalance: perceptive, creative, artistic
   d. Body imbalance: insomnia, popping joints, muscle stiffness
   e. Imbalance triggers: not following true self, eating on the run, spread too thin
2. Pitta
   a. Elements and qualities: fire and water, hard, sharp, light oily, liquid, spreading, sour, pungent, red, yellow
   b. Balance: discernment, sharp memory, joyful
   c. Mind imbalance: inflammation, hot flashes, skin rashes
   d. Imbalance triggers: overworking, eating while angry, overheating
3. Kapha
   a. Elements and qualities: water and earth, heavy, slow, cool, oily, damp, smooth, sweet, salty
   b. Balance: gentle, emotionally stable, endurance
   c. Mind imbalance: fearful of letting go, set in ways, depressed
   d. Body imbalance: obesity, congestion, excessive sleeping

e. Imbalance triggers: sedentary, emotional eating, emotion storage

Eight Constitutional Acupuncture: According to Eight Constitution Acupuncture (Medicine), a Korean yogic system, there are eight constitutions based on the strength of various physiological functions, including autonomic nervous function, metabolic function, and rhythmic function of the heart and lungs. I describe each below, paraphrased from an article in *Invitation to Health* (19 February 2020), by Dr. Hyonna Kang, "Personalized Health: Korean Eight Constitution Medicine". The eight are Hepatonias, Pulmotonias, Pancreotonias, Renotonias, Colonotonias, Cholecystonias, Gastrotonias and Vesicotonias. What's nice about this system is that it describes the potential problems and presents solutions. Note that some of the solutions involve eating meat and dairy. You can avoid those by substituting foods with similar health benefits.

Hepatonias have strong liver function but weaker lung function. They are generally robust and muscular. When healthy, they have higher-than-average blood pressure and tend to sweat, which is natural. Filling the lungs with oxygen by mountain climbing or cycling is beneficial, as are warm baths or a sauna. On the other hand, speaking at length exhausts the lungs and leads to fatigue. The liver produces bile that needs to be used to digest dietary fats. If Hepatonias overeat seafood, a vegetarian diet, or not enough meat, they feel lethargic and their facial complexion may darken.

Pulmotonias have strong lung function and a weaker liver function. They can sing or speak at length but are generally not muscular. They feel weak after sweating, so sunbathing and vigorous exercise leave them fatigued. On the other hand, swimming invigorates them because it keeps the skin cool. When eating meat and wheat, they may suffer from allergies, inflammation, or skin problems such as atopy. Vegetables, seafood and a gluten-free diet are beneficial for Pulmotonias. Pulmotonias must carefully choose any medication because the liver's detoxifying function is weak. They should also moderate alcohol and caffeine consumption.

Pancreotonias are prone to an overactive pancreatic and gastrointestinal function, but the function of the kidneys and adrenals is weaker. This leads to higher levels of gastric acid, a sensitive stomach and a tendency to constipation. Pancreotonias need to take care of what they eat. Spicy food, lamb, chicken, ginger, wasabi and alcohol can give rise to heartburn and increase the risk of peptic ulcer, diabetes, weight gain, high blood pressure, anxiety, inability to relax, and sleep disorders. Weak adrenals increase the risk of lower libido, infertility, prematurely greying hair and aging skin. The good news is that a suitable diet alone has many benefits: healthier skin, easier weight control, better blood pressure and improved libido. Iced drinks, fresh seafood and vegetables, pork, beef, and vitamin E benefit Pancreotonias. Sweating (running, sauna, sunbathing) is good for them, but they should avoid cold baths and swimming.

Renotonias have strong kidney function but weak pancreatic and digestive function. They are exhausted by overheating through vigorous exercise, sunbathing, and hot sauna, whereas swimming is beneficial due to temperature regulation. When they sweat a lot during the summer season, they feel drained and weak in their digestive function. Renotonias generally have poor circulation, exacerbated by cold food, iced drinks, beer, barley, cucumbers and pork. On the other hand, various spices, lamb, chicken, beef, cinnamon, ginger, garlic, spring onions and spicy food promote metabolic activity and circulation, warming their usually cold hands and feet. Foods or supplements containing Vitamin B are beneficial for them.

Colonotonias have a strong large intestine function but weaker gallbladder and liver function. As a result, a gluten-free diet low in fat and dairy is important for their health. Sushi/rice, green leafy vegetables, clams, iced drinks, hot chocolate, cucumbers, grapes and vitamin C are all beneficial. They should avoid meat, wheat, coffee and alcohol. A meat diet can adversely affect the immune function of the intestines, making them susceptible to inflammation and more serious conditions such as Parkinson's Disease, Multiple Sclerosis and Dementia. Chronic constipation or diarrhea is an early warning sign for deterioration of their health. Colonotonias need to be careful when taking medication such as antibiotics because the liver is slow to remove toxins from the body.

Cholecystonias have strong gallbladder function but a weak large intestine function. They tend to be athletic, have a good appetite, and have frequent bowel movements, typically 2-3 times a day. A diet including beef, pork, grains and root vegetables promotes circulation and stamina. They also need vigorous sports activity, or they can suffer from constipation. If they consume a lot of seafood, they will often feel abdominal discomfort and experience chronic diarrhea. They need to keep the abdomen warm, so drinking beer or swimming in cold water can result in diarrhea, high blood pressure and respiratory problems.

Gastrotonias have an overactive stomach and pancreas, but weaker bladder and kidney function. Foods further promoting hyperactive digestive function (such as spicy food, hot food, greasy food, lamb, chicken, garlic, ginger, cinnamon, curry, tomato, oranges, apples) not only cause digestive problems but can also result in anxiety and autonomic function imbalance in the long run. This constitutional imbalance can manifest as indigestion, constipation, chronic headaches, skin issues and sometimes whole-body pain. They should be cautious of side effects from medication (such as antibiotics). Alcohol and swimming in cold water are not beneficial. Fresh and cool foods and drinks can help counterbalance their overactive digestive function. A glass of cold or iced water in the morning and mixed grains (e.g., rice, barley, red bean, foxtail millet) would reduce overactivity in the stomach. At the same time, pork, seafood (blowfish, monkfish, prawns, crab, oysters) and vitamin E are beneficial for Gastrotonias' weak kidney function. When Gastrotonias are on the right constitutional diet, they tend to maintain good health on their own, so they usually have less need for visits to the doctor compared to other constitutions.

Vesicotonias have strong bladder/kidney function but weaker stomach/large intestine function. Their health is closely related to digestive processes. For example, if they eat many cold foods, their already low stomach function gets further weakened. Indigestion becomes the root cause of chronic illness, from gastrointestinal dysfunction to psychological issues due to phlegm-dampness accumulation in the body. They can easily compromise their health in the summer season because frequent sweating and cold food intake weaken their digestive function. Small meals, warm foods and less sweating are helpful guidelines for Vesicotonias to maintain good health, especially in the summer. Gastroptosis is the signature disorder of Vesicotonias. Profuse sweating and diarrhea drain their energy and make them feel fatigued and weak. They should eat small meals throughout the day, rest after meals (but not fall asleep), avoid cold food and drinks (pork, barley, cold beverages), prevent sweating, avoid the sauna and shower with warm water instead of hot water.

Feminine versus Masculine Energies: Polarities propel the Universe—yin-yang, up-down, light-dark, left-right, hate-love, feminine-masculine. The push-pull of opposites makes us bump into each other and learn from the experiences. It forces us to find ways to get along and our body cells to function in unity. Only when you experience this can you find individualization; you have to individualize before you find unity. Human beings are filled with polarities, and it's their overall karmic goal to balance them. Balance stabilizes the universal energy. Balanced energy propels ascension and helps everything and everyone return to The One. The One is the universality of everything. Our return to this is the ultimate goal.

Feminine versus masculine energies are polarities, and everyone has both. They're one of the internal push-pulls we need to work through. But what are those energies? In a spiritual or energetic sense, being male or female isn't physical. You can be a biological female with predominately male energy and vice versa. I am impressed with the gender-neutral people who intuitively know their energy predominance and prefer to self-design based on that understanding. Many of us are born with a balance, but that balance is quickly challenged by external stimuli, igniting the polarities and creating new challenges. The ratios we are born with aren't permanent. They are influenced by our family, school, faith group, friends, and greater energies around us. The United States, for example, is a masculine country which constantly challenges those with balanced or predominantly feminine energies. The relationship between them becomes unbalanced. The ratio isn't permanent.

I was born with a 60/40 masculine-to-feminine energy ratio. As I was growing up, my mother's energies were balanced on a scale yet in continuous conflict. My father was 90/10 at my birth and 80/20 at his death. I am now 40/60 because of my Lightworker practice. Although that looks like an imbalance, it's a non-polarity imbalance. Lightworkers don't need to seek balance. We want a higher feminine energy because it represents the more peaceful, loving universe of the 5D that we are moving toward to help others do the same. We had to evolve to 50/50 and then work toward 1/99. Yes, I (we) am periodically challenged by masculine energies, but we recalibrate through energy protection systems, meditation, energy work and creative arts activities.

How can you tell which energy is which? Pure feminine energy is creative, receptive, fluid, allowing, empathetic, sensual, emotional and nurturing. It is also more connected to spirit energy. The feminine energy flows and changes like the water of a river.

Pure masculine energy is focused, logical, stable, goal-oriented, strong, structured and driven. It is relatively detached from spirit as compared to feminine energy. Masculine energy is more like a rock than the water that flows around it.

The key to your energy balance is to watch how you feel about yourself and gauge your feminine and masculine interests. It's okay to be a physically-male star quarterback (strong, driven, goal-oriented) with a part-time Reiki energy practice (fluid, allowing, empathic, nurturing). It's okay to be a physically-female interior designer (creative, sensual) who also coaches a men's soccer team (goal-oriented, logical). Your body is only a physical vehicle for learning. It isn't meant to limit who you are or your interests.

Balance and peace between the energies is important. It's the key to unlock the door to higher energies.

Masculine energy dominated the planet until the first century CE (give or take a few hundred years). Even if a woman ruled—and many carried predominantly masculine energy—the masculine part got the applause. Over the last 2,000+ years, the Christ Consciousness energy started breaking apart the imbalance, bringing more feminine energy into play. The masculine energies fought back to keep things as they were, and the history books are full of stories of diasporas, holocausts, country takeovers, wars and inquisitions. All of that effort was to control the feminine energy. By controlling the energy, the male energy beings could control us. For the last 2,000 years, we've been trying to balance the energies and grow into feminine energy.

Foods and activities have masculine and feminine energies. Fruits tend to be feminine; vegetables bend masculine. Meat is masculine. Vegetables, exercise and self-assertion are masculine. Yoga, meditation, positive thoughts and words, gratitude, Reiki and Jyorei are all forms of feminine energy. After assessing your balance and deciding to get into balance, you can choose the right foods to help get you there.

Color Language

English is a language. Mandarin is a language. Music is a language. Color is also a language. Understanding color language's basics is important because it is fundamental to our design as beings, and the colors communicate with each other. Just as we work with masculine and feminine energies, we need to do the same with color. Consequently, we should be aware of the colors inside us to maintain our health and build our vibration.

You're already familiar with some aspects of color. Color symbolism has been used for centuries to show different emotions, ideas and thoughts. Pink means female. Blue means male. Green means nature and harmony. Colors have also been used to distinguish classes of people from another: blacks versus whites; blues versus reds. The Victorians of the 19th century associated colors with specific flowers and then assigned meanings. A white rose signified purity. A red rose symbolized passion.

Color symbolism is a simplistic way to say, "We understand that colors have some kind of meaning, and these are ours." In 4D/5D worlds and beyond, colors aren't things nor symbols;

they are vibrational frequencies. Violet, for example, has the highest vibrational frequency, and red light has the lowest which is why the former is a color associated with royalty, the latter with anger.

Does that mean that if we want a higher vibration to ascend, we should eat a lot of eggplant skin because of its violet color? Surface logic says "yes", but the true answer is "no". There are a lot of factors in the puzzle in which color is only one. But it certainly can't hurt (unless you're allergic to eggplant).

Our bodies are a conglomeration of color rays. The rays came together and created our forms. Each color collaborates with the other yet each is distinct. Distinction is difference. Difference creates polarities. The karmic goal is to combine them into a single high vibration and create an internal rainbow. The film *The Wizard of Oz* was more than a good fairy tale. It was a roadmap. It was popular because people were intuiting a way to their purpose while watching.

One way to bring the colors together is to consciously incorporate them into us. Think of it like bringing the family together for dinners, outings and movie nights while encouraging togetherness, love and unity. With colors, we can do this by eating, wearing, hearing, studying, seeing, smelling, feeling and experiencing them. We know this intuitively, and it is one of the reasons we enjoy flowers, art and kitschy things.

Which colors do you need more than others? You want colors that make you feel good and that you are lacking. A medical intuitive or Lightworker might be able to tell you, but you can do this on your own. Simply intuit it. What are you attracted to? What makes you feel good? What colors are lacking in your environment? What food is your body craving, and what colors do they bring you? Eat salads and dishes with a variety of colors. Be mindful of the colors speaking to you in the grocery store and elsewhere.

Color has phytonutrients to keep your body healthy, too. Plant foods contain thousands of natural chemicals called phytonutrients or phytochemicals. They are natural chemicals in plant food. "Phyto" refers to the Greek word for plant. These chemicals help protect plants from germs, fungi, bugs and other threats. Fruits and vegetables contain the highest number of phytonutrients. Unlike the vitamins and minerals provided by plant foods, phytonutrients aren't essential for keeping you alive. But eating or drinking phytonutrients can help prevent disease and keep your body working correctly. More than 25,000 phytonutrients are found in plant foods.

The phytonutrients are in the colors. The more colorful the plant, the more phytonutrients there are. The more color variety you can get, the healthier your body can be because you need the rainbow incorporated inside to lift your energy. The various phytonutrients also diversify your disease-fighting army.

Phytonutrients are rarely listed on nutrition labels, which is why we don't think or know about them. Many processed foods lack them, but other foods are rich in them, you just don't know about it. Dr. Greger of Nutritionfacts.org reported in a video that the more colorful fruits and vegetables have the most phytochemicals (25 November 2011). There are thousands of flavonoid phytonutrients in fruits, vegetables and other whole plant foods. The darker the color, the more they have.

He reported on a study indicating that phytonutrients may delay the onset of Alzheimer's disease. The study looked at the effect of drinking fruit juices. About 1,800 older individuals were followed for eight years. The subjects were asked if they drank juice, what kind and how much. When the researchers looked at the juices' nutrition labels, a lot of sugar was listed but not many listed nutrients. Those who drank fruit and vegetable juices—two that were higher in phytonutrients—regularly had a 76% lower risk of developing Alzheimer's.

There's another way to manage your colors: chakra balancing. I briefly introduced chakras earlier, but I will go into more detail here. If one or more gets clogged or out of balance, your color vibrations are impaired. Phytonutrients can be helpful, but a quicker and more effective tool is to realign and rebalance each one.

The word chakra comes from the Sanskrit word meaning "wheel", alluding to the vortex of swirling energy residing in each chakra's location. There are several different chakra energy systems within and around your body, and range from seven to 114, but we are referring to the central system up and down the spine. Each has a unique vibrational frequency and healing potency. There are seven main chakras within you, vertically aligned from your spine's bottom to the top of your head like a tower. We often see them represented as a string of globes or colored lights. The eighth through twelfth chakras are outside our bodies, stacked to the heavens above. If one chakra is clogged or malfunctions, your energy flow is blocked or irregular, possibly causing physical, psychological and/or energetic damage.

For the sake of discussion, I will focus on the seven main chakras Lightworkers read, align and heal. Each chakra vibrates a different color, the lowest vibrating at the base of the spine. Each subsequently-higher chakra has a higher vibration. I will explain each below in ascending order starting at the bottom and working upwards. I will present the color, location and meaning.

1. The first chakra is red, located in the region of the first three vertebrae, bladder and the colon. Its meaning is stability, security, safety and basic needs.
2. The second chakra is yellow, located from the navel to the breastbone. Its meaning is creativity and sexual center; creative expression.

3. The third chakra is yellow, located from the navel to the breastbone. Its meaning: personal power.
4. The fourth chakra is green, located at the heart center. Its meaning? The connection between matter and Spirit; serves as a bridge between our body, mind, emotions and Spirit; our love and connection source.
5. The fifth chakra is blue, located in the throat and mouth areas. The meaning is the source of verbal expression and the ability to speak our highest truth.
6. The sixth chakra is indigo, located between the eyebrows (also known as "the third eye"). Its meaning is center of intuition.
7. The seventh chakra is violet, located at the crown of the head. Its meaning is enlightenment and spiritual connection to our higher selves, others and the divine.

Years ago, I knew I had internal physical and emotional issues manifesting in weight gain, emotional tension, creative blocks, and feeling out-of-sync. If you're having any physical or psychological issues, the problem could be due to one or more out-of-balanced chakras. I suggest you find a Lightworker you trust and have them take a look. That's what I did. I went to a series of energy healers practicing chakra balancing, Jyorei, and Reiki to balance my energy. I also tapped meditation, yoga, exercise, positive thinking, and intuitive eating to help. The package of practices did the trick. I rely on all of them (and diet) to stay aligned.

Eating Locally

Doorstep Foods: Most of this book is about consuming energy through one means or another. Regarding eating, we discussed that some foods have more energy and higher vibrations than others and that preparation matters. But the geographic origin of the food is also a factor. Tropical fruits have a higher vibration than other fruits because of their higher absorption of the Sun's rays. However, if you live in Cleveland and the fruit is shipped from Central America, that local apple might have more vibration. To help you understand, here's a little quiz. I'll also provide the answers.

Suppose you're of South Korean ancestry and living in Cleveland, Ohio. Does a Granny Apple from Sandusky, Ohio, have the same vibration as a Granny Apple grown in Valle de Guadalupe, Baja California, Mexico? No. The Sandusky apple will have a higher vibration because it was grown closer to you. It has more of the family high vibration resonance. The apple also didn't have to travel a long distance, exhausting some of its value.

Does a cherry tomato from your garden have more vibrational energy than a cherry tomato gifted to you from your neighbor's garden? Yes. Your garden is closer to you and has your energy.

For a New Yorker, does brown rice grown in South Korea have a higher vibration than brown rice grown in Northern India? No. India is geographically closer to New York City.

The system is this: Plants grown closer to your residential doorstep will have a higher vibration than plants grown farther away. "Doorstep" has two meanings. The first definition means anything grown in your yard or on your land. The farther away the plant grows, the less energy it will have when it arrives on your plate. The second definition is ancestral, which I will get to later. First, we'll focus on physical proximity.

Why Local? There are three reasons to eat locally, all about maximizing vibration. Please note there are nonvibrational reasons to eat locally, such as supporting local farmers and protecting the environment, all equally good reasons. But this book is about vibration for ascension, so I'll focus on that aspect.

The first reason is relational. The plants from your property know you personally and are there to serve you. Your vibration spreads across the area, and the plants perceive its presence, love and support. And like your human genetic family, they appreciate you, know you and want to give back. Local plants also have a broader devotion to serving the people in that immediate community, too, and you are a member of that community. If you live in Dayton and you're visiting Phoenix, the Phoenix plants will support you when you visit, just like you would do for visitors in your home. The plants put oxygen in the air to breathe, food to nourish your system and beauty to make you smile. But the Dayton plants are your family, so their love and vibrations are higher for you, just as the Phoenix plants are for Phoenix residents.

The second reason is travel distance. The longer a fruit or vegetable travels from its source, the lower its vibration when it arrives on your plate. The Costa Rican apple loses vibration from the uprooting, the travel, the packaging, the waiting in the port and the gassing it goes through to ripen. In contrast, if you pick an apple from your front yard and eat it immediately, you'll get the highest vibration possible.

The third reason is seasonal. Foods grown in their natural seasons will have a higher vibration than those grown off-season; local foods tend to be seasonal. If it's December in Cleveland, and you bought a four-pack of corn-on-the-cob at Heinen's, it's out-of-season corn from a greenhouse or somewhere south of the border. It's still safe to eat. It simply means it will have a lower vibration.

How do you know what's in season? You can go online and do a search, or you can rely on your experiences. I grew up in farm country, so I had a sense of season, but I later moved to California where seasons operated differently and the foods were different. Google became my source, as did the local farmer's market. Growing up, however, many of our foods came from our garden, the fruit trees, or local roadside stands. "What is available in which season" wasn't a question I ever asked because I automatically knew. I loved corn on the cob and always mourned the early fall when it was no longer available. But pumpkin and apple season made up for it. Of course, the seasons will vary geographically. Southern California has a longer growing season than Ohio for similar foods. Nonetheless, a season is a season.

Local Foods? How do you define "local"? Well, it sometimes depends on who you ask, so I'll give you some common parameters and you can decide for yourself. These are based on a literature review and the opinions of various organizations.

A Locavore is a person whose diet consists only or principally of locally grown or produced food. Locavores posit that a 100-mile radius is local. Indeed, 100 miles qualify. A radius that size has a unified climate and soil conditions, so it makes sense. But can local be even farther away?

Most believe that anything within 250 miles is local. There will be climate similarity, of course. Still, there can also be variations based on various factors such as proximity to an ocean, mountain, desert, or if you are going north-to-south. Regardless, differences will be minor. The distance equals a five-hour drive in the car, allowing me to get there and back in one day by car, making it feel local. It's certainly more local than the next suggestion.

A US 2008 farm bill stated that a product may be transported up to 400 miles from its origin and still be considered a "locally or regionally produced agricultural food product". A group of growers and corporate farmers were behind the decision, and who could blame them? People prefer local products, and the growers have products to sell. If you can legally put the word "local" on the package, the buyer will think, "Wow, grown on a farm in the valley over there." I live in Los Angeles, and San

Francisco is about 383 miles away. Nobody here considers San Francisco local. I lived in New York City for 20 years before moving to Los Angeles. Anything outside of the five boroughs and first-ring counties was considered nonlocal. Pittsburgh was 390 miles away, and nobody in New York thought Pittsburgh was local.

As you can tell, there is diversity around the definition with each group hard-and-fast on their position. The vibrational test is "The closest to your door has the highest", and that is what you need to know.

How do you know if a plant you're buying was locally grown? Sometimes, the origin is posted on a sign at the grocery store or a price sticker. Of course, what does "local" mean—400 miles, 250 miles, 100 miles? If you purchase it at a local farmer's market, the Food Co-op, or a store that says, "Locally grown produce, only," it's probably grown within a 100-mile radius. All I can suggest is to do the best you can and eat as close to your doorstep as possible. Eating an apple from Oaxaca is still better than eating a side of beef from the farm next door.

Chapter Seven

Spirit, Mind and Body

Overview

Spiritual nutrition is about vibrational energy. Food is one source, but there are others equally important. Those include (but are not limited to) forgiveness, gratitude, mindfulness, stories, positivity, prayers and usefulness. Each contributes to raising and maintaining your vibration. They're like the parts of a machine, in a way.

There is an overlap between the practices because they are all about flow. You can think of them like components of a soup—broth, veggies, grain, seasonings, etc. They have separate identities, yet they are all parts of the nourishing soup.

The stories we tell ourselves and others will sound like mindfulness. Gratitude includes forgiveness. Yoga includes exercise. Etc. The practices help you build a higher vibration through various approaches with nuances, but each practice has its place. I do them all, and as I grow up, I may discover new ones. Without introducing reductionism, I'd miss something.

While reading, remember a quote from Dr. Joel Fuhrman, MD. He's a board-certified physician specializing in preventing and reversing disease through nutritional and natural methods. Fuhrman authored six books, including *Eat to Live*.

Here is what he has to say: "Medicines cannot drug away the cellular defects that develop in response to improper nutrition throughout life." This is so very true. Once the cells and your DNA are altered, they don't automatically return to their original state. If you were an alcoholic for 30 years, eating higher vibrational foods will help, but you will have to find new ways to work around the changes created by excessive alcohol consumption.

The same is true for vibrational energy. I encounter many clients (or client wannabes) who think I'll cure them if they just come for a chakra balancing or Reiki session. Others rely on religious rituals. But if you spent much of your life eating poorly and ignoring your spiritual being, the process created a different you, and you will have to work with that you. Chakra balancing won't erase everything. You'll need a comprehensive, long-term investment in energy practices, including healthy eating.

Forgiveness

How It Works and Why: You are a 3D human living physically and energetically in a 3D world. You will make mistakes. Everyone makes mistakes. We can't get around it. Sometimes the mistakes are accidental. Sometimes they're intentional. Sometimes we make them; sometimes, others deliver theirs to us. The question is: How do we handle mistakes when they come our way from others? If we didn't forgive each other, we'd each be at constant war. Constant war would not only destroy everyone and everything, but it would significantly lower our vibration, and that's not our purpose on Earth. Forgiveness is essential for vibrational development.

In May 2021, I was riding my bike in my lane down Santa Monica Boulevard in West Hollywood, a suburb of Los Angeles and an entertainment hub. I love the scenery along the way: West Hollywood Boy's Town, Beverly Hills mansions, Century City, West LA, Downtown Santa Monica and the Santa Monica Pier. It is a terrific round-trip four-hour ride and a good weekend workout. On this particular day, the weather was perfect: 75 degrees F, sunny skies and no wind. Yes, I was wearing my helmet. Yes, I was obeying traffic laws.

I was early in my journey from Hollywood, mindful of the parked cars along the street, watching for the warning signs of a door flying open. After I crossed Fairfax, a car came up from behind me on a slow-moving section of the street. I felt her right front fender on my side and her side-view mirror banging against my arm, shoulder and side. Usually, that would have been okay (it's happened before), except her mirror didn't fold over. I got hit square-on, and I went to the ground, dazed.

I'm a "get up, get up, don't let this get to you" kind of person, so I pushed myself up. As I rose, I saw the car's driver coming toward me and was grateful that she had stopped. Many people who hit cyclists and pedestrians don't stop. I checked my moving parts, and everything seemed to be working, albeit rigidly, and I was bruised and scraped. I was greatly relieved because it could have been much worse.

She apologized profusely and looked so sad. I felt terrible for her and wanted to assure her that I was okay. I forgave her immediately, told her I'd be fine, and then walked my bike back to the car and went home. I didn't even get her name or her license number. It didn't occur to me to do it. I was fine, I thought.

An hour later, I could tell that something was wrong. I had a huge bulge on my side where the car hit, and my arm was swollen. I self-admitted to the hospital, where I assumed I'd be treated and released but was held there for five days. Fortunately, no bones had to be repaired. I didn't require surgery. I refused all pain medications, and I didn't budge in my forgiveness to the young woman. Eventually, my body recovered, and I returned to normal.

My forgiveness was reflexive, and I'm glad I did it. Karma will take care of her in the end, and my forgiveness helped that happen. Relieving your karmic debts is critical for advancing your soul and lifting your energy. If I'd held resentment, it would have lived inside of me, eaten away at my peace and stopped me from learning the lessons I needed to learn. It would have also retarded my recovery, lowered my vibration and fed my fears. My forgiveness of the driver also helped her karma. She had lessons to learn and needed a clean channel in which to learn them. My forgiveness lifted both of us.

Forgiving someone doesn't mean that what they did was okay or they got off the hook. It also doesn't mean that you have to start (or continue) liking the person. It merely means that the malicious string between you and the wrong-doer breaks at the point of forgiveness. You've cut the tie. You're free to move on. It isn't yours to live with.

Here is another example from a different angle. It uses a bag of potatoes to teach forgiveness. I discovered this story on social media and loved it. The story is about a 10-year-old boy who admired his teacher because she was always so happy. He wanted to learn why she was always happy.

"I'd like to be happy like you," he said. "Can you teach me?"

"Certainly," she said.

"What do I have to do?"

"I want you to find an empty potato bag. I'm sure you can get one at a grocery store or from home. Carry it with you all the time, even when you sleep. Make sure it never leaves your side. Every time someone hurts you, put a potato into the bag."

"Okay," he said.

He went home and explained this to his father, a single parent. His father gave him a potato bag from the trash. Whenever someone hurt him, the boy put a potato into the bag. He carried the bag everywhere. Eventually, some potatoes rotted, and the bag got too heavy to carry. He went to his teacher and complained.

"You see," she said. "If you're not happy, it's because you're carrying all the bad things you experience. And like that bag of potatoes, it becomes too much. Those bad things that happen to you rot inside you, and you become unhappy. So, treat your

Spiritual Nutrition

life as if it were that bag of potatoes, and forgive them every
time somebody hurts you." She pointed to the bag. "When you
forgive them, you don't put a potato into the bag."

"But how can I forgive them?" he asked. "They were mean
to me."

"They're carrying their own bag of potatoes. People have
been mean to them too, and they're unhappy. When people are
unhappy, they are mean to others."

"Oh," he said.

"So, starting today, whenever someone is mean to you, think
of that bag of potatoes of yours. You don't want to put a potato
into the bag, so imagine the person as having been hurt. As I
look at that bag at your feet, I can tell that you understand what
it means to be hurt, so you can forgive them just like you would
want the same if you hurt someone else. Then, move forward."

How to Forgive: Forgiving others and yourself is simple: You
do it. If you're still angry later, do it again and again and again
until the pain goes away. I incorporate forgiveness into my daily
meditative practice. Sometimes, I pull out my journal and write
down the names of the people who hurt me, and then I forgive
them in writing. I do the same with myself for the wrongs I
committed, new and old. Other times, a memory of someone
who had been mean to me will pop up, and then I forgive them.
Sometimes, that person is someone I'd forgiven earlier, but the
reoccurring negative feeling tells me I'd better try again, so I do.

When we forgive them, we're cutting the cord between us,
keeping the memory alive, and letting them live with what they
did without feeding off of ours. We're doing this to free ourselves
of the pain of anger, a vibration-lowering activity. Forgiveness
doesn't make it right; it just severs the tie so everyone can heal.
In meditation, when you forgive yourself, cut the cord with the
person and apologize to them and move on.

Many Zen Buddhists have a prayer called Gatha of Atonement. They chant it before a meditation sitting. They use it because nobody can remember every harmful thing they've done to themselves and others through the years, and things keep coming up.

All karma ever committed by me since of old,
Due to my beginningless greed, hatred, lust, envy and delusion,
Born of my actions, speech and thought,
Now I atone for it all.

If you feel this will work for you, borrow it and amend it to fit your needs.

Gratitude

Why Is Gratitude Important? Expressing gratitude and feeling grateful are essential for maintaining a connection to Spirit and raising your vibration. Ungratefulness is a lower energy form, and we all know how hard it is to be around an ungrateful, complaining person. Sometimes, my head hurts listening to them. Being ungrateful disconnects us from Spirit, lowers our vibration, creates physical illness and feeds unhappiness. The lower energy radiates out, affecting everyone around us. The opposite is true for grateful people, which is why we prefer to be around them.

Gratitude is the act of thinking, feeling and communicating appreciation for the people, circumstances, and material possessions in your life. Expressing gratitude and feeling grateful are two of the most effective ways of getting in touch with Spirit and the greater Universe. It tells the Universe you want more of what you're grateful for, and then you get more. When you appreciate something, your 3D ego moves out of the way because you can't focus on your ego and express appreciation simultaneously.

Expressing appreciation and being thankful provide natural fertilizer for physical and spiritual health. They reduce depression, lower blood pressure and increase your energy and happiness. They also make you more likeable, trusting and socially adept.

This Hasidic folktale summarizes it well. It's a paraphrased version from MindfulTeachers.org.

"Two rabbis were collecting donations. When they approached a wealthy man, he only gave them half a penny. One of the rabbis was offended by this paltry offering, but the other thanked the man and blessed him.

A little while later, the man approached them with an apology and a silver coin. Again, the first rabbi thought this was a very small donation from such a wealthy person, but the second rabbi thanked him and said, 'You are a good and generous man.'

The rabbis went on their way, and a little while later, the rich man ran up to them, heaving a heavy sack. He apologized again to the rabbis for not giving them more money sooner and handed them the sack full of silver coins.

The first rabbi was amazed, and the second rabbi explained what happened: The rich man had been quite generous with donations, but one day a beggar approached him when he only had half a penny in his pocket. The beggar was so rude in refusing this small sum that the rich man was offended and decided to only give away half-pennies to anyone who asked him for money.

The rich man's negative attitude was reinforced by the scorn with which recipients rejected his half-penny offerings. But when the rabbis thanked him for his gift, the rich man felt appreciated, and he remembered his better self and returned to his previous generosity."

Gratitude goes a long way, and here are ten simple things you can do to express it:

1. Begin your day by saying out loud, "Thank you for giving me another day. It'll be a terrific one." Do this right after you wake up and before leaving your bed. Make it the first thing you think of and the first thing you do.
2. Find reasons to be grateful. Thank the kitchen table for being your workspace. Thank the handcrafted soap in the bathroom for cleansing your skin. Thank the slippers on your feet for keeping your toes safe and warm.
3. Thank the food you eat before you eat it and mean it. It's quite a blessing to have it. Many people don't have enough food. And when you think of the journey those plants went through to feed you, wow. How could you not be grateful? A simple, "Thank you, plants, for nourishing me," is enough.
4. Before meditation, say "thank you" to your ancestors, spiritual guides and others. Say "thank you" for the opportunity to have this lovely space for meditation, the lit candles, the comfortable chair or cushion, etc.
5. After meditation, thank your spirit guides for being with you during meditation and staying with you throughout the day.
6. Thank the people, animals, etc., who help and teach you. This includes the beings who are unkind to you. Their reaction to you is also a lesson.
7. Thank every positive and challenging experience you have during the day for helping you learn and grow.
8. If you drive a car anywhere, thank the car for transporting you and the road for supporting it. Thank the trees along the street for sucking up the pollution.
9. Extend appreciation to the cosmos at the end of each day for everything that happened, from when you got up to when you went to bed.

10. Keep a gratitude journal. It also lets the Universe know in a bolder way that you are thankful.

Meal Prayers: Prayers are a form of gratitude, but I mention meal prayers because they differ from other prayers. I'm not talking about the kind of prayer you learned to say at church or elsewhere, where you focused on thanking your God. Those are fine, but you may want to think broader. I'm talking about the kind of thoughtful prayer for the entire trail of travel that brought the food to you. With this kind of prayer, you also thank the plants you're eating, the people who grew and delivered them, the Earth for growing them and the Universe for providing all you need. Your gratitude is felt by the entire chain, which lifts everyone and everything along the chain. It also adds value to the vibration of the food in front of you.

I've run across a few meal prayers that I think work well. You can try them and see what fits. They are nondenominational. This one is my favorite:

Thank you, Angel of Disarmament, for removing any harm to me that may be in this food.

Thank you, Angel of Enrichment, for enriching this food for my benefit.

Thank you, plants, for giving your life for me and contributing to my good health.

Thank you to everyone and everything over the billions of years who brought this food to my table.

I also like the one from the Soto Zen Buddhist White Plum Lineage. The lineage has before and after meal prayers, but I especially like the before prayer. There are some very-Buddhist things in here, but you get the idea.

*Let us reflect on the efforts that brought us this food and consider
how it comes to us.*

*Reflect on our virtue and practice and whether we are worthy
of this offering.*

Regard greed as the obstacle to freedom of mind.

Regard this meal as medicine to sustain our life.

For the sake of enlightenment, we now receive this food.

First, this food is for the Three Treasures.

*Second, it is for our teachers, parents, community and all
beings everywhere.*

Third, it is for all beings in the six realms.

Thus, we eat this food with everyone.

*We eat to stop all evil, to practice good, to liberate all beings,
and to accomplish the Buddha way.*

Mana Force

Mana is another word for life-force energy. It's also an impersonal
source of external and internal energy in people, places and
objects. You can transmute it to protect yourself from NPs. You
can also use it to ask your Higher Power for things you need.
Mana comes from the same source as Reiki — the central Sun —
but a Reiki Master must attune you to use the energy. Mana is
available to anyone and doesn't require attunement. The user
draws the energy from their surroundings.

You will read in many sources that mana force energy is the
miracle-working secret of Hawaii's Kahuna priests, the authors
claiming that the priests had exclusive knowledge and use.
Many authors also declare they are revealing the energy to the
public for the first time. Truthfully, mana has been around for
centuries. Jesus of Nazareth reportedly used it. Yogis use it. The
Celts used it. And now, you can use it.

The most common technique used to gather mana is the one I learned from Brian Scott, author of *The Reality Revolution* (2020). He took steps two through seven from Madeleine C. Morris' book *Miracle of Mana Force: Secret of Wealth, Love and Power* (1975). I added step 1 because it seemed to go more smoothly when I did. It was also easier to create an energy shield around me.

1. Stand if able. If not, sit upright with your feet flat on the floor.
2. Prepare your mind by imagining a nature scene or place you love, and spend time with it until negativity and doubt leave you.
3. Exhale, and then go through a series of quick, punctuated exhales until all the air is gone. You want to free yourself of negative air.
4. Take a long, deep breath, filling first at the diaphragm and then the lungs.
5. Hold your breath for as long as possible and fill yourself with mana energy.
6. Repeat the breath cycle two more times.
7. Hold your hands out facing each other.
8. Repeat the breath cycle three more times, filling with even more energy.
9. Expand the energy out six feet beyond you on all sides. This is your protective shield.
10. Bring down the Sun's energy and infuse it into your energy bubble.
11. Thank the Sun and your Higher Self.

Meditation

What Is Meditation? Meditation is about training yourself to be aware and having the opportunity to observe yourself and your thoughts without judgment. It's a process of putting you in touch with all that is as you go within yourself. It connects you to something universal and makes you an ambassador to the Universe. Meditation helps you become present by enabling you to rest in the here and now, where you can fully engage with whatever you're doing in the moment.

An objective of meditation is to become "mindful". Mindfulness is the mind's quality and power that's aware of what is happening without judgment or interference. We become more aware of where we are and what we're doing without becoming overly reactive or overwhelmed by what's happening. It includes being thoughtful and aware of our bodies, feelings and things around us. When we are "aware", we see and experience the Universe beyond our 3D ego's limitations. Things are no longer about or for us; they're about or for everything. Mindfulness also helps us see with more clarity and serenity. A cluttered mind depletes our energy, lowers our vibration, and clutters the lives of others.

Mindful practice is bringing one's attention to the present moment. The mind's habit is to shuttle between reflecting on the past and worrying about the future. This causes us to miss what's going on in the present. It also creates disconnection from Spirit, a situation fed by the attention paid to television programming, computer and phone screen addictions and electronic games. Those activities can be fun and educational, but mindfulness is difficult to accomplish when you are distracted or addicted by these external things.

When we practice mindfulness, we create space for ourselves—space to think, breathe and form our reactions. Creating this space is my primary meditation goal. I also try to do the same throughout the day, taking time to stop and notice things, cutting vegetables intentionally, pausing to listen to the rhythms of the wind and rain, etc. When we do this, the Universe can communicate with us. It opens a direct channel to help lift our vibration.

Meditation's Benefits: Mindfulness meditation has many more perks. Meditation has become so widely practiced that left-brained scientists now study it without mockery, including the Cleveland Clinic, doctoral students and The Eco-Institute (to name a few). The researched benefits could fill their own book.

The Cleveland Clinic states that meditation can have beneficial health effects by decreasing the negative impact of chronic stress on the body and mind. Meditation can support physical and emotional well-being by reducing muscle tension, quieting the mind and reducing anxiety and stress, all things that raise our vibration.

The work of a Stanford University doctoral dissertation supports those benefits. A dissertation is an extended, written treatment of a subject submitted as a final step toward earning a Doctoral Degree. A literature review is the portion of the dissertation summarizing what we already know. The student's work was comprehensive and, in my opinion, represents my experiences and understanding. According to the review, meditation can boost your health by increasing immune function, decreasing pain, decreasing inflammation at the cellular level, boosting happiness, increasing positive emotion, decreasing depression, decreasing anxiety and reducing stress. All of those things lift your vibration. Meditating within a group can boost your social life, increase your sense of connection to others, increase social connection and emotional intelligence, and make you more compassionate and feel less lonely.

The Eco-Institute researches through intuition, vibrational experience, and literature reviews of spiritual material. The Institute posits that meditation is "the very best positive energy and vibration raising tool." The Institute is an Earth sanctuary and learning community dedicated to healing the human-Earth relationship. Their educational farm and regenerative sustainability learning center reside on 28 acres in the Piedmont of North Carolina, eight miles west of Chapel Hill.

Meditation helps us remember that we are all in this thing together. When we start seeing ourselves in others, a miraculous thing happens: Everyone becomes their other self. Others are you in another form and on another timeline. No matter your current path, we are all returning to Source. Meditation is the key to this path and effectively removes any self-imposed limitations currently preventing your dreams from manifesting into reality. The inner calm and stillness of mind brought about by meditation shift your vibration to a higher frequency, making you a permanent magnet for positive experiences, setting your life on the highest and best possible course.

How to Meditate: The purpose of meditation is to quiet your mind enough to connect to Spirit, even if just for a few seconds. There are lots of ways to connect. You can meditate sitting down, standing up, walking around and doing chores. I even meditate when I drive, feeling the steering wheel with my hands, noticing the sunrise and feeling my feet on the pedal. You don't have to sit quietly. You can do mini-meditations throughout the day by just stopping for a minute, taking a deep breath and then going inside. You can stop and spend time admiring a flower, petting an animal or even washing the dishes.

There are many ways to meditate, and a single method doesn't fit all. The key to meditation is practicing every day, whether easy or difficult. If all you do is five minutes, start there and sit for longer when ready. Eventually, you can sit quietly for an hour or two.

Most kinds of meditation include these four common elements:

1. A quiet place where you are less likely to be interrupted.
2. A comfortable position.
3. A focus of attention such as your breath, a word or phrase (sometimes called a mantra), or an object.

4. An open and nonjudgmental attitude toward the process, thoughts or anything else that gets in the way.

Most who meditate develop their system. If the four suggestions above don't help, perhaps you can find a partner and work together. You may also want to engage a teacher or an organization for more structured instruction. If you go this route, I suggest you lean away from secular teachers and toward those offering meditation as a spiritual practice. Many Tibetan, Soto Zen and yoga centers will teach you. Most provide free instruction online via Zoom or YouTube. All you need to do is start.

Mindfulness

Mindfulness is the mind's quality and power that's aware of what is happening without judgment or interference. As stated in the previous section, we become more aware of where we are and what we're doing without becoming overly reactive or overwhelmed by what's happening. It includes being thoughtful and aware of our bodies, feelings and the things around us. When we are "aware", we see and experience the Universe beyond our 3D ego's limitations. Things are no longer about or for us; they're about or for everything. Mindfulness also helps us see with more clarity and serenity. A cluttered mind depletes our energy, lowers our vibration, and clutters the lives of others.

Mindful practice is bringing one's attention to the present moment, which is an objective of meditation. When we aren't mindful, we miss what's happening in the present. A lack of mindfulness also creates a disconnect from Source.

If you're looking for a good example, I'd suggest viewing *The Monkey Business Illusion* (2010). The rabbi's wife showed it to us at a holiday event. As I write, the video lives on YouTube. The video asks you to count the times a ball is passed between the female players. Your ego drives you while you're counting because you want to win and get the correct number of passes. This activity cuts you from mindfulness. While you're counting, half of the viewers miss the fact that a gorilla steps in and then leaves. Over 80% miss the changing of the background curtain. They miss these things because they're focusing on counting the throws and not the bigger picture of what's happening. Practicing mindfulness enables you to see everything.

Again, when we practice mindfulness, we are creating space for ourselves, and creating space is my primary meditation goal. I also try to do the same throughout the day, taking time to stop and notice things, cutting vegetables intentionally, and pausing to listen to the rhythms of the wind and rain. When I do this, the Source communicates with me. It has a direct channel to help lift my vibration.

But how do we practice mindfulness? I borrowed these steps from Mindful.org because they were clear, accurate, and relied on meditation, the practice that opens the door to day-long mindfulness. I paraphrased and tweaked it, but these six activities summarize what the site had to say.

1. Find a place to sit that feels calm and quiet to you.
2. Set a time limit. It can help to choose a short time if you're beginning, such as five or ten minutes.
3. Notice your body. You can sit in a chair with your feet on the floor, you can sit loosely cross-legged, in lotus posture, you can kneel—all are fine. Just make sure you are stable, and in a position you can hold for a while. Relax your body parts from the feet up, feeling each part as you relax it.
4. Feel your breath. Follow the sensation of your breath as it goes in and out.
5. Notice when your mind has wandered. Inevitably, your attention will leave the sensations of the breath and

wander to other places. When you notice, return attention to your breath. It might help to "count" your breaths from one to ten and then repeat. Counting is a good distraction.

6. Be kind to your wandering mind. Don't judge yourself or obsess over the content of the thoughts you find yourself lost in. Just come back. Even the most experienced Zen Monk has to work to quiet their mind.

Storylines

"The most important of all factors in your life is the mental diet on which you live. The food you furnish to your mind determines the whole character of your life." This quote is from Emmet Fox's book *The Seven Day Mental Diet*. Fox (1886-1951), author of nine books, was a New Thought spiritual leader of the early 20th century, primarily through the Great Depression, and his words still ring true. You are who you say you are, a practice many rich and famous used to get where they landed. To learn more about this approach, read Napoleon Hill's *Think and Grow Rich*, Malcolm Gladwell's *Outliers* or Franklin Covey's *The 7 Habits of Highly Effective People*.

So much is about the stories we create about who we are, how we built our lives, and where things are today, providing the framework for how we see the world and ourselves. These stories can feed the NPs and lower our vibrational frequencies. It's a hidden thing that creates unhappiness, makes it difficult to change our habits, creates relationship problems, and feeds frustration, anger and disappointment.

The hidden thing is the stories we tell ourselves. These stories aren't lies; they're based on our beliefs. They're narratives that we construct based on our experiences, a perspective on the world around us and an interpretation of facts from our perspective. And that's the key: "from our perspective."

Each of these examples has very different stories about the same situations — it's about which details you pay attention to and how you shape the narrative of the details. Psychological distress often has roots in a story. Here are stories I heard in a TED Talk by Lori Gottlieb, a psychotherapist. She writes an advice column called "Dear Therapist", so she gets many stories. I'm paraphrasing here:

> I got an email from a woman distressed because her husband had been distancing himself from her for a little over a year. They've been married for ten years, but they haven't had sex for that long, and she found a woman's phone number on his phone to whom he makes frequent calls. She did an online search of the woman and found that she worked with him and was very pretty. Should she leave him? They have a long history together and two children. She doesn't want to hurt the children.
> (Gottlieb, 2019)

To illustrate the power of stories (Gottlieb often hears both sides), she created a counter-story from the husband's perspective, and it went something like this:

> I don't know what to do with our marriage. We've been married for a long time, but she hasn't been supportive since my father died 14 months ago. She seems more distant. I feel like we are strangers in the house, and I'm worried that the children are being hurt. I turned to a coworker who had recently lost her father, too, and she's been a lifesaver. She's been easy to talk to and makes me feel better. What should I do about my marriage? I don't want to keep going like this.

From their perspectives, the stories are correct, but their stories keep them apart. The separation creates distress affecting everyone around them, including their children, yet they perseverate on their versions without coming together and understanding each other.

Some stories stay with us forever, and we adopt them as truth.

Throughout the day, you're telling yourself and others lots of stories about what's going on, how wrong other people are, or how good or bad you are at things. What you seed colors your view of everything, putting you into a negative feedback loop. Here are a few examples:

I can't declutter my home, I'm just a messy person.

My husband can't cook. He can't even unpeel a banana. I don't let him into the kitchen.

I can't get in shape; it's not my thing.

My teenage son wouldn't eat vegetables as a toddler, so I stopped feeding them to him. It keeps peace in the house.

I can't be brave, I'm a worrier.

My best friend comes from a dysfunctional family, and that's why he is so argumentative.

I can't quit smoking, I've tried.

My challenge to you is to start noticing what you're telling yourself about everything, even if the story makes you happy. If the story makes (or keeps) you unhappy, it's lowering your vibration. So, start to become aware of your stories, good and bad. Notice them throughout the day. When we become attached to a story, it's hard to become unattached, but becoming aware of being hooked is the first step.

What can we do if we're hooked on a story? It can be challenging to break out of the story trap. It happens to all of us. The story seems so natural that you can't let it go.

The first step is awareness. When you tell a story, stop and recognize it. You can even see it as a dream — it's there, but it isn't real. It's just a thing you created, right or wrong.

The next thing is to sit with the story. Notice how it's making you feel, including your body's physical sensations. You don't have to do anything; just be aware. Bring yourself into the present moment, label it as a story, determine how it affects you, and look for the other side of it. Once you recognize the story and you can see to the other side, revisit it to make it more positive and hopefully truer. Don't forget that the new story is still a story, but at least it doesn't hurt you anymore. You may need to revise it later as you learn more.

The new story could be simple, moving from "I can't be brave, I'm a worrier," to "I'm working to be braver, I'm making progress, and I'm learning." If you're in a relationship with someone you love, and things aren't going well, sit with that person, listen to them without comment, and work to understand their side of the story. Once you do, you'll reexamine your story and change it to reflect what you've learned. The goal is to move from negativity to positivity and the world of possibility.

Positivity

The word "positive", in psychological and spiritual terms, means looking towards the good side of things. It is an attitude that helps you see the good in people and yourself rather than the negative and the failures. A positive attitude is a state of mind that envisions and expects favorable results. It also manifests in the willingness to try new things. Even pretending to be positive is better than being negative. Positivity increases vibrational frequency; negativity lowers it. If you want to increase your vibration energy, you'll want to be naturally optimistic. Since the objective is to raise your vibration, you'll want to find a way to remain naturally positive.

If you need a visual, view Emoto's work and see the effect of negativity on those crystals.

To become more positive, you'll need to recognize when you're about to be negative. Negativity is a tendency to be downbeat, disagreeable, and skeptical, expressed and thought. Yes, in thought, too. Just because you don't say the words doesn't mean your thoughts aren't conveyed. This is a world of energy in which we are all "one". Your thoughts travel between people through your aura to theirs and then intuitively read on the other end. People's physical eyes see things, too.

Here's an illustration of what can happen in this situation. For example, two of your employees are late for work, and you're frustrated. They missed the first ten minutes of a morning meeting, causing you to rearrange the agenda. You don't know why they're late, and you try to be understanding inside. Was it traffic? Negligence? A family emergency? Despite your effort to be thoughtful, you're still angry. After the meeting, you approach them with a pretend smile, sweet words and clenched fists. They apologize, and they feel bad. They carpooled to work, and there was an accident on the 110 freeway. Yes, they should have called, and they will the next time.

Faking optimism and happiness on the inside helps you, but it doesn't help others. Your thoughts and behaviors sent a negative message in overdrive. Why? First, because your politeness was intentionally false. Others can intuit what you're feeling; your fists reinforce the belief that you're angry, and lying about your feelings is the sucker punch. You've deflated everyone's energetic vibrations while co-creating a prolonged fear that has resulted in their future secrecy about work matters.

Employee tardiness is a grievance issue for those of us who supervise employees. For those of you who supervise others, I assume your hairs are already rising on your back. When I worked for a social services agency, I had an employee who was chronically late for work. I usually didn't arrive at work until an hour after he was expected to come, so I didn't know if he'd been on time or late unless someone told me. One day, the Executive Director learned that he was chronically late. She was furious about it and asked me to correct it.

Knowing that I needed to care for my vibration and his, I took a deep breath. He was a human soul, a sentient being, and a recent college graduate. A full-time semiprofessional job was new to him, and he had much to learn about work. He was the Volunteer Coordinator, but for the first hour of every day, he was our opener and sat at the front desk of a building that included our childcare center. If he were late, the parents were late to work or school. I wanted to be careful with his energy: He was still young in the Earth school, and I didn't want to hurt him. I imagined the circumstances that could make him late—personal negligence, family responsibilities, car troubles (he had a beater), etc.

I had my conversation with him in his office later in the day to make it less intimidating for him. I entered his space with complete empathy, assuming he didn't want to be late, something was making him late, and we were going to find a solution. I began with pleasantries and a kind introduction, and the conversation went something like this. I am using fictitious names to protect the guilty.

"Evelyn (the Executive Director) mentioned that you were late this morning. What happened? Can I help you in some way?"

"I'm sorry. I was only ten minutes late. Where I last worked, the start time was dead set. I didn't realize it was dead set here."

"I can understand that," I said. "I've worked at places like that. The problem here is that some of our parents need to drop their children off and rush to work, so they aren't late. If we open the doors even one minute late, it can affect them. So, starting tomorrow, can you arrive five minutes early to ensure the door is unlocked and you are at the front desk?"

"Yes, certainly," he said. "I'm sorry. It will never happen again."

"No problem. I'm glad we cleared this up."

He appreciated my approach, and we resolved the issue peacefully. I later learned that his lateness was due to poor planning: He had to be at work to open the doors at 7:30 a.m., but he often got up at 7:15 a.m. (he lived down the street). I chuckled about this inside because I need at least two hours to get ready for work—meditation, breakfast, clothes ironing, etc. Once we solved the lateness problem (he vowed to get up ten minutes earlier), I worked with him on career development. He was only late one other time in the next three years, and he'd texted me to come in: His father had a heart attack and he was in the hospital with him. I was happy to go in and take his place until he could get to work.

Negativity's roots are often in self-fertilizing unhappiness, a pessimistic attitude that usually expects the worst. Someone with negativity as the default focuses on the thorns in the holly bush versus the Sacramento-green leaves and the cherry-red berries. When a negative person hears a newborn child cry, they'll see it as a nuisance rather than an awe-filled opportunity to experience a new life.

Another thing driving negativity is the belief that honesty should be punishing. Whenever I hear someone say, "Well, I was just being honest," I can see and smell the negativity without knowing what they said. Being honest, to them, is cloaking their negativity with a lie of goodwill. It's a form of revenge, not honesty. This type of negativity is the easiest to recognize but not always the easiest to cure. But if you want to express yourself in ways that lift everyone's vibration, here are some steps.

First, sit back and try to understand this from their perspective. If you want a model, you can use the one I gave to my tardy employee: stop, assume the best, try and figure out the best, and enter the conversation as a resource-mate versus an intervener.

Second, ask yourself, "Honesty according to whom?" A good illustration of this is the story I told in the last chapter section about the couple having marital problems. I showed how there were two entirely different perspectives of the same situation. Before addressing the issue, you'll want to learn what happened from the other person's perspective. The only story you know about this is yours, but what makes yours right?

Third, ask yourself, "Why am I doing this?" Before talking to my employee about his tardiness, I wanted to clarify to myself how his tardiness affected our families. I didn't want to make it about the work rules or my need for perfection. I examined the real purpose of his work and put the focus there. While exploring the reason, you may discover that your real motive is to please your ego, which you don't want to do. You want a common good reason. If you can't do that, say nothing.

There are various reasons for our negativity—physical ill-health, mental illness, karmic circumstances, conditioning at school or home, media exposure, influencer behavior, and entity possession. The reasons are too numerous to list. What's important is to recognize that negativity is an addiction: Before you can correct your own, you should acknowledge the problem, distance yourself from the sources, and employ the tools in this book to become more positive. As you emit positivity, you will draw positivity to yourself, your vibrational energy will increase, and your life will improve. You will also be able to deliver your honesty in a way that lifts everyone's vibration.

Being Useful

Giving back to your community comes from an inborn desire to be a part of lifting the world around you. It's a selfless act with a higher vibration. The aid you freely give, from a service-to-others mind, spreads the vibration between you, the helped and the broader Universe. You heal those you help while healing yourself.

According to an article in *Psychology Today*, scientific research indicates that people who help others from the heart—meaning from a service-to-others position—tend to be healthier and happier (Marianna Pogosyan PhD; 30 May 2018). Pogosyan wrote:

> For instance, the well-being-boosting and depression-lowering benefits of volunteering have been repeatedly documented. As has the sense of meaning and purpose that often accompanies altruistic behavior. Even when it comes to money, spending it on others predicts increases in happiness compared to spending it on ourselves. Moreover, there is now neural evidence from MRI studies suggesting a link between generosity and happiness in the brain. For example, donating money to charitable organizations activates the same (mesolimbic) regions of the brain that respond to monetary rewards or sex. The mere intent and commitment to generosity can stimulate neural change and make people happier.
> (Pogosyan, 2018)

Helping from a service-to-self position has the opposite effect. If you help to change another person for your gain or to prove your worth, you deliver a lower, draining vibration. I'm sure you know how that feels when people do that to you. Do you remember the people who "helped" you by racing in and doing things for you when you said, "No, I can do it on my own"? Or the ones that helped, believing they were better and wiser than you and had to show you because you were inferior? You experienced icky feelings from those circumstances. The icky feelings were lowered vibrations.

One of the best examples I've seen of people claiming to help others through a service-to-self position was through my work as a nonprofit fundraiser. Most of my examples come from nonprofit board members at work. Every board member will tell you they're there for the mission, but the truth for many is more complicated. A nonprofit board of directors is the nonprofit's governing body. Board members are supposed to focus on the organization's high-level strategy, oversight and accountability. Their responsibilities contrast with employees or managers who oversee the nonprofit's day-to-day operations.

In a recent position I held at a nonprofit in Los Angeles, it was my job to work closely with individual board members to encourage them to follow through with their promises. Each member signed an understanding of their role and function. Some of those promises included giving a minimum amount of money per year, buying tickets to events, attending meetings, serving on committees, etc. Some board members did everything; some did nothing; some did a few things. Those who did everything tended to hold the organization's mission in their hearts and were there primarily for service-to-others reasons. The members who did less tended to be there for service-to-self reasons. They were there for public recognition, to "set this place straight", or to secure the nonprofit as a customer.

In my first year, we got two new board members: a banking executive and a retired engineer. The banker had served on several boards prior, coming on and off of them about every three years. His purpose for joining the board was to show his customers the bank's community responsiveness and to secure the agency as a customer. He was required to serve on a committee and give or get $3,000 for the agency. He did neither. When encouraged to do so, he left the board.

The other new board member was retired and looking for something to do. Fortunately, he served on a committee and gave his annual cash gift. He also believed he could improve the agency through his high-level skill. This board member left because he thought the other members wouldn't listen to his wisdom.

Neither new board member understood or felt the mission. They were good people but too far removed and service-to-self oriented to engage. They were also argumentative at meetings. It felt icky to be around them.

We did have good board members, and my favorite one was a longtime member. She attended every meeting with hugs and smiles, gave her annual gift, pitched in and volunteered. She also helped acquire large cash gifts from other sources. She helped acquire much-needed in-kind items such as water bottles for the 5K fundraiser race, grocery bags for the Thanksgiving and Christmas food giveaways, and winter coats for the clients. She brought more to us than any other board member and lifted everyone. We widely appreciated her, and we felt good in her presence. Her service-to-others orientation made her crave usefulness, and we all benefited from it.

Chapter Eight

Going Vegan

The Next Step

Exercise, yoga, meditation, positivity, usefulness, etc. Okay, you get it. But eating only plants? It's an important pillar of the vibrational formula. With the other tools, you can hit a wall that an unhealthy body will create. You will also miss out on all the communication from plants that you won't get from the other tools. You can ascend by eating meat, dairy and eggs, but it will be more challenging and less likely. You will want to make your body into a healthy energy conduit.

"Slow down, dude," you're saying. "I've been eating animal products all my life, and I love them. Everyone tells us that animal products are healthy and that we'll get sick if we don't eat them."

We'll have to agree to disagree on the sick part, and I mentioned some of the health issues that led me to this conclusion. Of course, if you have a karmic reason for eating animal products, you should eat them, but I'm guessing that most readers don't have this karma. Regardless, everyone would be better off eating more fruits and vegetables, so perhaps that could be your goal. Besides, if your body needs animal products today, it doesn't mean it will require them tomorrow or next year. This book presents a "better, better, best" system. The Fifth Dimension is about energy balance, and animal products put your energy out of balance. If you're trying to transition to vegan or include more plant foods in your day, I offer some suggestions below.

First, I recommend setting an ultimate, amendable goal and giving yourself room to reach it without a rigid timeline. Some people can make this change immediately; others may take years. I took years. It's hard to know how long it will take at the beginning, but it doesn't matter; just get started. Remember that the path to the ultimate goal will likely be crooked as you move along. You'll probably end up taking five steps forward, three steps back; four steps ahead, four steps back; ten steps forward, six steps back. The process isn't linear for most of us.

There are at least two approaches to getting started: (1) jumping in without looking back and (2) going gradually. Choose whichever you think will work for you. If you try one and it doesn't work, try the other. You can always go back and forth between them. I tried both approaches over time. Back in the olden days, when I was less mentally mature, I was a diver because I thought perfection was the virtuous route. After all, I told everyone I would do this, so I will do it. After failing more times than I could count, I realized the ultimate goal was important, not the speed of approach.

When you set your goals, be careful not to set them like New Year's resolutions, things most people break. You don't want to label yourself a failure because you didn't meet your goal. I can't tell you the number of people I see on vegan social media sites who beat themselves up because they discovered an animal product in their food or craved fish and ate a piece. It was like their action was a crime, and they should be given the death penalty. Many of them subsequently give up for fear they'll do it again. Some of the best advice I can give is not to let temporary setbacks stop you. Pick up where you left off and try again. Create flexible-enough short-term goals to make them attainable and adjust them as you go along. If you were teaching a seven-year-old to bake a dozen cookies, you certainly wouldn't set the goal of a perfect dozen on the first try. You'd break the tasks down into doable steps, and if something went wrong, you'd still praise the child for what he accomplished and try again later. It would help if you gave yourself the same break.

It took me 20 years to become entirely vegan. I began as an on-and-off-again pescatarian, then an on-and-off-again vegetarian, and then an on-and-off-again vegan. Once I became vegan, I set a new goal: eat 90% raw plants. I'm not there yet, and I've been seesawing between 60% and 80%. I'm about 65% now, but my goal is still out there. I'll keep trying. Eventually, I will get there. I suggest the following stage process to start. You can amend it to fit your needs.

Stage One: No processed foods for 30 days. Processed was defined earlier.

Stage Two: Add to the above no red meat for 30 days.

Stage Three: Add to the above no chicken for 30 days.

Stage Four: Add to the above no fish and no added salt for 30 days.

Stage Five: Add to the above no cheese for 60 days (it may take longer to edge out).

Stage Six: Add to the above 30% raw, 25% fat consumption (max), for 60 days.

Stage Seven: Add to the above 50% raw, 20% fat consumption (max), for 60 days.

Stage Eight: Add to the above 70% raw, 15% fat (max), 40% protein (max), for 30 days.

Stage Nine: 80% raw, 12% fat (max), 40% protein (max), for 30 days.

Stage Ten: 100% raw, 12% fat (max), 40% protein (max), indefinitely.

Things Are Going to Change

Your health, relationships and vibrational energy will change as you progress. The changes will be automatic and anticipated. Healthwise, you'll be detoxing just as an alcoholic or drug addict might do. You've heard the stories about what they go through as their body cleans out and adjusts to being cleaner. You may even have similar experiences as your body cleans out the guck of your diet and your emotions. The two are intertwined.

The longer you followed a conventional diet and harbored conventional thoughts, the longer it could take you to detox, and the more intense the symptoms could be. I was lucky because I'd been a fresh fruit and vegetable eater for decades and had exercised regularly. Nonetheless, my body had its reactions that included numbness in my right foot, joint issues and itching. The result was clearer skin, thicker hair, more energy, brighter eyes and fewer aging signs.

I'm not the only one who experienced these things. I still see people in social media vegan groups ask, after a couple of weeks of trying, "How long is this going to take? I can't take it any longer." If I respond, I usually say that we all go through it, which takes as long as it takes. It's different for everyone. It took me two years.

It isn't just your body that changes. Emotions will surface. Relationships will change too, and you'll get more communication with your Spirit guides. Your energy vibration is speeding up and throwing off emotional, memory and physical illnesses. Much has been stored within you, held in place by a lower vibrational frequency. You've had disappointments, traumas, sorrows, joys, good fortune and memories. You can't have a higher vibration while holding onto the lower vibrational feelings and memories. Emotionally, the cleansing process may include bouts of depression, crying, nightmares and flashbacks. Don't try to push them back with lower vibrational activities such as unhealthy food, drink, drugs or self-doubt.

As your vibration rises and your friends' and family members' vibrations stay the same, you will see everyone differently, and they will see you differently, too. Some of your relationships will fade away. You'll also attract new ones. Some of those in your original circle will become testy. Some will improve.

Some relationships may have to end because the people (family, friends, coworkers) try to hold you back.

In some cases, you may have to be brave and end the relationship. I went through an upheaval in friendships, with some drifting away. My newer vibration just wasn't a match for theirs any longer. I also had to say goodbye to a family member who tried to keep me at a lower vibration. Fortunately, I met new people who were a higher vibration and a good match. Helpers also came into my life. I met a Lightworker who restored my DNA to fully functional and another who balanced my chakras. I wouldn't have met them had it not been for my vibrational changes.

Your higher vibration will provide clearer interaction with spirit guides, too. I started seeing light flashes and began receiving more Spirit gifts. I encountered more pennies and feathers in my path. I smelled smells from my past that nobody else smelled. I heard my old cuckoo clock on the wall chiming after 30 years of silence. I found plastic leaves on my living floor when I had no artificial plants in the apartment. After a meditation, I received a printed white restaurant napkin at my feet in my Brotherhood of Light initiation at the Modern Mystery School. It wasn't there when I first closed my eyes, but it was there when I opened them, and nobody had put it there. The paper napkin had Japanese lettering, so I took it to a Japanese friend to read. It was from a shop in Japan that sold a comfort food noodle that Japanese people enjoyed. I framed it and put it on the wall in my living room.

On and on. So be prepared, because you never know what's going to happen.

Communicating with Lower Vibrational Humans

Raising your vibration and going vegan will recreate the world within and around you. The relationships will change, and new people will enter your life to disrupt you. People can see that you are changing, and most 3D people are wired to keep things the same. Your light is brightening, making you a bigger target.

Remember that opposing yang forces will always exist for your new yin behaviors. It's part of the universal design. Healthy vegan eating is yin, and the yang will rise when you step into it. It's how the Universe is designed at the 3D level. Regardless, you live in a world of 3D people, so you need some tools to deal with them. Don't take any of it personally; none of it's personal. It's about them, not you. But opposition is understandable, considering we've been facing it for thousands of years. Systems to oppose spiritual development are well-practiced and automatic. We've talked about protecting yourself psychically, but here are some tools to deal with opposition over your food choices.

Conventional Vegans: Believe it or not, there's even a little war within the vegan community. There are various viewpoints on vegan eating, and some are adamant about their positions. I call them Conventional Vegans, a term I invented for those who follow a traditional path and fit one or both of these categories:

1. vegans who ignore (or don't understand) the health aspects
2. vegans who see veganism as a religion

My friend calls the health ignorers "French Fry Vegans" (FFVs). FFVs eat vegan, but their diets include many processed foods loaded with salt, oil, sugar and chemicals. Some see the foods (e.g., cheeses and meats) as "the" vegan foods. They mean well, but they'll assume you want the foods because they want them. They may challenge your decision to set them aside. If you challenge their practices, you should expect pushback.

Those who see veganism as a religion have lines drawn on what to eat and do. If you step over their lines, you will hear from them. If they step over those lines, they have intense guilt. Some religious vegans oppose raw juicing and the fruitarian approach, for example. Some are anti-raw. When I went 90% raw, I got considerable pushback on social media from a few people, and I had to block them. There are many reasons for this, but I'll mention two.

First, those who deadlock on religious vegans are often deadlocked on other things. The stability of a religious structure provides the rhythm of their world.

If you interrupt that world, you interrupt that rhythm.

Second, the opposer knows your choice is healthier, but they can't do it themselves. Maybe they tried, failed and gave up, or perhaps they refused to try. Their medical doctor may have told them to eat plants to restore their health, but they can't. Either way, they turn on the yang and create a war with spiritual vegans. It's a form of what psychologists call "cognitive dissonance". Cognitive dissonance is the state of inconsistent thoughts, beliefs, or attitudes, especially regarding behavioral decisions and attitude changes. A mental conflict occurs when beliefs are contradicted by new information. This conflict activates areas of the brain that manage personal identity and emotional responses to threats. This causes these parts of the brain to shut down and ignore what they hear because it disregards the potential evidence that contradicts what they believe is "the truth". The opposing forces are inside them, fighting each other and coming out to fight you. Fighting helps them diminish the dissonance through their efforts to restore their familiar world.

Nonvegans: Although most people will either say little or say, "Wow, I wish I could do that," there will be people who are not vegan who have something to say about your choice. The mere expression of opposition is in the range of pre-impolite to impolite. The most frequent reasons I hear fit into what I'll call "four collections".

1. The Natural Collection: Eating animals is instinctual; we have canine teeth to eat meat; eating meat helps us develop large brains; we've always been eating animals; animals eat other animals.

2. The Health Collection: Vegans aren't healthy; where do you get your protein; where do you get your calcium; where do you get your iron?

3. The Harm Collection: Vegans kill plants; killing animals humanely is okay; if we didn't eat animals, they would overpopulate the planet and starve to death.

4. The "Other" Collection: It's too extreme; vegan food is expensive; if we didn't breed animals, they wouldn't have a life.

You will hear all of these arguments with varying degrees of intensity. I recommend simply listening, saying nothing, and/or responding with, "We'll have to agree to disagree," which you'll want to say politely. Don't take the bait: These arguments are presented not to provide a logical argument but to start and maintain a fight. I wish I could say they mean well, but most comments lack supporting logic and are being presented to lower your vibration.

You'll have to live in this world and find ways to function without derailing yourself. You will never be able to convince them otherwise, so it's best to step away. In some cases, you'll be in inescapable situations and have to do something, such as at parties, family events, conversations with your spouse or partner, and the daily feeding of children. You may need some parameters and ideas.

At Parties and Events: I'm writing this section amid the holiday season when people come together for parties. These can be challenging events for vegans: We often have to go to events where we will be faced with unhealthy food choices and verbal opposition. Here are a few things you can do.

Negotiate with the hosts: If it's a work event, speak to the organizer or join the planning committee. If you can, suggest vegan-friendly foods. Sometimes, there's nobody to negotiate with in advance, or you may get a negative response when you try. Either way, be calm, bite your lip and don't add logs to the argument's fire. If it's a potluck, bring something vegan to share. You may also discover that others will, too. Not every dish has animal products in it. If you're sure there won't be vegan options, eat in advance.

I ran into a party situation today. I am a local professional organization board member, and we had our holiday social this afternoon. Usually, we're asked ahead of time if we need vegan options, but this time we weren't and I forgot to plan. Fortunately, there was a buffet where hotel employees dished out the food. The salad was my option.

At Family Events: First, let me define family. Family is whatever you decide it is. It could be blood relatives, the family of choice, a mix of the two or "other". Family members are people with whom you have an emotional attachment that you define as your family.

Now, onto your omnivore family members.

Whether you're attending a family dinner at your folks or a holiday event with extended family, the majority won't be vegan, and you will need to prepare or face questions and a growling stomach. Say something to the host in advance as a courtesy to prepare them. If you show up, you're not eating anything, somebody asks why, and the host finds out your diet choices, you could hurt the host's feelings. Most hosts want everyone to enjoy the food and be happy, and they'll usually find a way to accommodate you just as they would anyone else.

When you reach out, do it gently and carefully. Don't ask the host to prepare something for you or enter into a debate over veganism. When I've faced this, I usually say, "I'm a plants-only person. Is it okay if I bring a dish or two to share? I have some yummy recipes." That way, I tell them without asking them to do something special for me. That usually leads to a, "Sure, but I'll make some things for you, so don't worry." That's what you're looking for—thoughtfulness and kindness.

In some families, telling them you're vegan is like outing yourself as LGBT or Q. You know where your family falls on the spectrum. You may be jittery about telling them but extend the courtesy, regardless. You don't want "not" to eat anything and listen to people ask, "Aren't you going to eat anything? Aunt Mary went to so much trouble." Aunt Mary's going to learn about it, and it may hurt her feelings. If she's the accommodating sort, she's going to feel horrible that she didn't make anything for you. If you say something in advance, but you're sure there won't be vegan dishes, either eat before you go or bring food with you.

This "courtesy call" system goes for all family events involving food, including restaurant trips and vacations. You don't want to walk into a burger place as a treat from your father only to discover that you have no options. Your father will feel horrible, figuring he could have taken you somewhere else had he known.

Sometimes, you have an event to attend at which you have no influence. Maybe you and your spouse/partner are going to an event to which he was invited, and your spouse forgets to say something to the host. In that case, I recommend Buddha's approach. You don't have to be Buddhist to do this; it's the idea that counts. The Buddha suggested you eat what is presented to you because it's a gift. He posits that turning down a gift is far worse than sticking to your diet. Gifts represent the flow of loving-kindness, and you don't want to disrupt the flow. You can always (inside your head) thank the animals for nourishing you and apologize for the loss of their life. These gestures mitigate the damage.

I did this recently at a friend's birthday party. His friend hosted the party, and I was on the invitation list. Before I arrived, I'd already decided to apply the Buddha approach so I didn't insult the host. She'd gone to considerable trouble to produce this birthday party, and I saw the love flowing. The meal was paella, a dish full of fish and other meats, and the dessert had egg and dairy. My friend told her I was vegan, and the host profusely apologized. I told her not to worry. Her food was filled with love, and I certainly would make an exception tonight to eat the love. The dish was terrific, by the way. I'm still trying to figure out how to veganize it.

Your Spouse/Partner: Handling things at home can be more challenging than dealing with the public. At home, each family member has an equal right to their way of life, even the children. Sometimes, you're responsible for preparing their food, which can cause conflict if you're vegan. More often than not, there is tolerance and support, and sometimes the spouse joins you. Social media is full of posts by vegans saying, "My husband, the great omnivore, decided to do this with me." That's a sign of love.

What should you do with spouses or partners who won't support you? Here are a few suggestions.

First, don't try and convince them to join you. Let them be who they are. If you do that, they'll be more likely to let you do your thing without complaint. Maybe they'll come around later by watching how you grow. You never know.

Second, have them do their own cooking. Certainly, they'll eat some of the vegan foods you prepare, but they should buy their own food and cook it if they crave something else. If they can't cook, sign the two of you up for cooking classes. Yes, the cooking class won't be vegan, but that's okay. You'll still learn something, and your spouse will gain independence and self-confidence in the kitchen.

Third, buy a cookbook for your spouse or partner with basic recipes that match their eating habits. There are tens of thousands of cookbooks, so ask around for suggestions.

Fourth, begin gently exposing your spouse to veganism. Perhaps she/he/they could watch a film or a documentary with you and go to a vegan cooking class with you. Some of those classes will include preparing an entire meal that everyone eats together when finished. The quality and diversity of the meal could get their attention.

Fourth, agree on what to feed the children. The best thing to do, I believe, is to follow the desires of your children. That will best keep the peace with your spouse.

The Children: Today, many children push their parents to eat vegan versus the other way around. It's how a lot of parents began this journey. I see countless social media posts from parents asking what to do when a child refuses to eat animal products. Many more in the upcoming generation are Third Wavers coming in to help. They don't want the weight of animal products in their energy.

If the decision to go vegan is yours, and you've had your conversation with your spouse, and they say "fine", then present the vegan option to the children. The children love you, and many will try it out of love. Others will jump in. Others will look at you as if you have two heads. Again, follow their lead.

If your children are reluctant, you'll still want them to understand your choice and respect it. Who knows? They may come around to veganism later. Here are some ideas on how to help them.

First, include the children as kitchen helpers, teaching them how to prepare the foods. Children love to be independent, and eventually, they'll insist on making their own dishes.

Second, use baking as a tool. Kids love to bake cookies, so bake and decorate some vegan cookies together. The "fun" of the activity will draw them in. Then, after they try the cookie, they'll realize it's delicious and that vegan is completely doable.

Third, learn to make child-friendly vegan dishes. Maybe they still want meat and dairy, but that doesn't mean they can't eat vegan dishes. If you need some child-friendly recipes, do a YouTube search on vegan cooking for children and find a few sites you like. I recently saw one featuring a chocolate shake with a fistful of undetectable spinach. The drink was chocolatized with carob, sweetened with dates, thickened with frozen bananas and liquified with coconut water. I tried it, and wow, was it good.

If your child says, "Absolutely not. I'm not eating that vegan stuff"? Agree with the child, "You eat your food, and I'll eat mine." The meal will inevitably have a combination of vegan and omnivore foods, and the child will eat both. Simply give them time for now. No pressure.

Celebrity Vegans

Celebrities play a significant role in many people's lives because fans see them on the screen and relate to them. I don't watch television. I don't follow celebrities, and I rarely watch studio films, but I'm aware that many are vegan and vegetarian because they sometimes enter that world where I can see them.

Some people believe that if you go vegan, you won't have the energy or brain width to do what you want, but that isn't true, and these examples provide proof. I researched these people online and included their names and biographies below. It's a sample list—not a complete list of every vegan celebrity. But it's enough to prove the point.

I include artistically, cognitively and physically successful vegans. If you want to be a professional football player, it's doable. There are plenty of successful vegan performers if you want to be an actor or an actress. If you want to be successful in business or the sciences, there are vegans in those realms, too.

The celebrities mentioned below operate in various competitive and creative fields, from auto racing to opera; from pro basketball to the USA Army. Because I mention them doesn't mean that I approve of how they live otherwise, what they think, or of their type of work. I make no judgments about their choices, just as I don't make judgments about readers' choices. If there's a vegan celebrity mentioned who you think is a banana head, that's fine. The point is that they are successful while eating plants. Hopefully, you'll be able to relate to one of them.

Please note that I accumulated this information in 2020 and 2021. Some people mentioned below may have changed diets or philosophies since my online search. Please note that there are one or two vegetarians. There are no omnivores on the list.

While reading the biographies, I noticed variations in the reasons for their choices. Reasons mainly included intuition, concern for animals and health. Some of the vegans were vegetarians, first.

I break this chapter section into categories: Arts, Athletes, and Varied. Individuals are listed in alphabetical order by category.

In the Arts: *Chokeules*, otherwise known as Choke, is a Canadian underground hip hop artist and member of the Backburner crew. His real name is Justin Lepine. He is a former group member of Toolshed (with Timbuktu and Psyborg) and Swamp Thing (with Timbuktu and Savillion).

Alan Cumming is a Scottish entertainer who has contributed to several films, plays, and other works. He is currently well-known for his role in CBS's *The Good Wife* for which he was nominated for three Primetime Emmy Awards, two Screen Actors Guild Awards, two Golden Globe Awards, and a Satellite Award. He says he prefers to eat vegetarian because he does not like the taste or texture of meat.

Ellen DeGeneres is an American comedian, television host, actress, writer, and producer. She starred in the sitcom *Ellen* from 1994 to 1998 and has hosted her syndicated television talk show, *The Ellen DeGeneres Show*, from 2003 to 2022.

Legendary musician *Stevie Wonder*, who earned 25 Grammy Awards to date, made the decision to go vegan in 2016 for both health and environmental reasons.

Moby, an American musician, has been vegan since 1987. He first cut meat from his diet at age 19, thanks to his beloved pet cat Tucker. Moby told *Rolling Stone* he realized he "would do anything to protect him and make him happy and keep him from harm."

Athletes: *Meagan Duhamel* is a Canadian pair skater. With partner Eric Radford, she is a two-time world champion (2015, 2016), a 2018 Olympic gold medalist in the team event, a 2014 Olympic silver medalist in the team event, a 2018 Olympic bronze medalist in the pairs event, a two-time Four Continents champion (2013, 2015), the 2014-15 Grand Prix Final champion, and a seven-time Canadian national champion (2012-18).

Kyrie Irving is an American professional basketball player for the Brooklyn Nets of the National Basketball Association. He was named Rookie of the Year after being selected by the Cleveland Cavaliers with the first overall pick in the 2011 NBA draft.

Activist and athlete *Colin Kaepernick*, the professional football player who made headlines after kneeling to protest police brutality during the USA national anthem, is vegan. He made the connection between human suffering and animal suffering. A few years ago, he went vegan after realizing he couldn't support any forms of oppression, whether to humans or non-humans.

Mike Tyson is an American former professional boxer who competed from 1985 to 2005. He reigned as the undisputed world heavyweight champion and holds the record as the youngest boxer to win a heavyweight title at 20 years, four months, and 22 days old.

Venus Williams is an American professional tennis player. A former world No. 1, Williams was ranked world No. 1 by the Women's Tennis Association several times. Her sister, Serena, is also vegan.

Varied: Business, Social Justice, Science, Military, Religious:
Thomas Colin Campbell is an American biochemist who specializes in the effect of nutrition on long-term health. He is the Jacob Gould Schurman Professor Emeritus of Nutritional Biochemistry at Cornell University and the principal author of *The China Study*. Campbell has become known for advocating a low-fat, whole food, vegan diet.

The Dalai Lama is the exiled Tibetan Buddhist spiritual leader. He is vegetarian, although he eats meat when hosts offer it.

Albert Einstein was a German-born theoretical physicist who developed the theory of relativity, one of the two pillars of modern physics. His work is also known for its influence on the philosophy of science.

Coretta Scott King, the wife of Martin Luther King, advocated for Black equality. She also believed that compassion should extend to animals. Dexter Scott King, her son, convinced her going vegan was the next logical step to living a nonviolent lifestyle.

As the CEO of Whole Foods Market (now a subsidiary of Amazon), *John Mackey* was a vegetarian for three decades who converted to veganism. He also operates a diet of three organic vegan meals per day.

Chief Warrant Officer 2 *Jeremy Patterson* (CW2 Patterson) has been making news waves for initiating the first vegan menu at a USA military dining facility. Under Patterson's lead, the Guns and Rockets Dining Facility at Fort Sill, Oklahoma, now has vegan options at every meal. Patterson has been a Food Advisor for a little over two years at the 75th Field Artillery Brigade, with several years of experience as a Food Advisor and 17+ years within Food Service in the Army.

Russell Simmons is an American entrepreneur, record executive, writer and film producer. He is chairman and CEO of Rush Communications, co-founded the hip-hop music label Def Jam Recordings and created the clothing fashion lines Phat Farm, Argyleculture, and Tantris.

Resources

I consulted many sources on the journey to this book, and I list as many of them as I remember. I include resources for cooking instruction, foraging, meditation, mindfulness, plant life, vegan health, raw foods, spiritual eating and the New Earth. I hope you find them helpful.

Cooking Instruction

Hundreds and hundreds of books, websites and YouTube sites offer recipes and cooking instructions for cooked and raw vegan dishes. However, most of them use salt, oil, sugar and processed foods. The ones listed below either don't use them or use them minimally. The sites are also free.

Cooked

Butterfly Effect Plant-Based Weight Loss, https://www.youtube.com/channel/UCgTuVYt2UoejqZt5u2Bqz1A

Chef AJ, https://www.youtube.com/user/therealchefaj

Harshdeep Swami, https://www.youtube.com/c/HarshdeepSwami

Jane Esselstyn, https://www.youtube.com/channel/UCkVtuE3WR0NhNnDiP5d_pAA

Mic the Vegan, https://www.youtube.com/c/MictheVegan

NutmegNotebook, https://www.youtube.com/c/NutmegNotebook

Plant-based Gabriel, https://www.youtube.com/c/PlantBasedGabriel

Raw

FullyRawKristina, https://www.youtube.com/user/FullyRawKristina

JoeCross, https://www.youtube.com/user/FatSickandNearlyDead

Lissa's Raw Food Romance, https://www.youtube.com/c/RawFoodRomance

Okraw, https://www.youtube.com/user/okraw

Raw Natty N8, https://www.youtube.com/c/NateMaris
The Healthy Life, https://www.youtube.com/user/Markus Rothkranz

Foraging

Books

Baudar, Pascal, *The New Wildcrafted Cuisine*, 2016.
Baudar, Pascal, *The Wildcrafting Brewer*, 2018.
Slattery, John, *Southwest Foraging*, 2016.
Vorderbruggen, Mark "Merriwether", *Idiot's Guide to Foraging*, 2015.

Meditation

Books

Chodron, Pema, *How to Meditate*, 2007.
Hanh, Thich Nhat, *Being Peace*, 1987.
Hanh, Thich Nhat, *How to Sit*, 2014.
Hahn, Thich Nhat, *Taming the Tiger Within*, 2005.

Websites (as of 2022)

David Scharff, https://www.linkedin.com/in/davidscharff/
Modern Mystery School, www.modernmysteryschoolint.com
Philipp Schardt, http://philippschardt.com/
Sat Devbir Singh, www.satdevbir.com/
Zen Center of Los Angeles, www.ZenCenter.org

Mindfulness

Books

Bowen, Bill, *A Complaint Free World: How to Stop Complaining*, 2007.

Chozen Bays, Jan, *Mindful Eating*, 2009.

Cousens, Gabriel, *Creating Peace by Being Peace: The Essene Sevenfold Path*, 2008.

Edwards, Betty, *Drawing on the Right Side of the Brain*, 1979.

Emoto, Masaru, *The Hidden Messages in Water*, 2004.

Fox, Emmet, *The Seven Day Mental Diet*, 1935.

Glassman, Bernard and Rick Fields, *Instructions to the Cook*, 1996.

Goldsmith, Joel S., *The Infinite Way*, 1947.

Hanh, Thich Nhat, *The Art of Mindful Living*, 1991.

Hanh, Thich Nhat, *Old Path, White Clouds*, 1991.

Hanh, Thich Nhat, *Savor: Mindful Eating, Mindful Life*, 2010.

Hawkeye, Timber, *Faithfully Religionless*, 2016.

Merullo, Roland, *Breakfast with Buddha*, 2007.

Zenji, Dōgen, *Tenzo Kyōkun* (Instructions for the Cook), 1237.

Documentaries and Videos

The Earthing Movie, 2019.

The Monkey Business Illusion, https://www.youtube.com/watch?v=IGQmdoK_ZfY&list=WL&index=21

Plant Life

Books and Articles

Buhner, Stephen Harrod, *The Secret Teachings of Plants*, 2004.

Burbank, Luther, *The training of the human plant*, 1906.

Cowen, Eliot, *Plant Spirit Medicine*, 1995.

Esperide, Ananas, *The Music of the Plants*, 2014.

Grossinger, Richard, *Plant Medicine: Origins*, 2013.

Hewen, Ross and Howard G. Charing, *Plant Spirit Shamanism*, 2006.

Lanese, Nicoletta, "Plants 'Scream' in the Face of Stress", *LiveScience*, December 6, 2019.

Mancuso, Stefano, *Brilliant Green*, 2015.

Ninkovic, Velemir et al., "Aboveground Mechanical Stimuli Affect Belowground Plant-plant Communication", *PLos One*, 2018.

Powers, Richard, *The Overstory*, 2018.

Website (as of 2020)

Damanhur, www.damanhur.org

Plant-based Health

Books

Airola, Paavo, *Worldwide Secrets for Staying Young*, 1982.

Barnard, Neal, *Reversing Diabetes*, 2006.

Batmanghelidj, Fereydoon, *Your Body's Many Cries for Water*, 1992.

Breuss, Rudolf, *The Breuss Cancer Cure*, 1995.

Cafaro, Bob, *When the Music Stopped: My Battle and Victory Against MS*, 2015.

Campbell, T. Colin and Thomas M. Campbell, II, *The China Study*, 2005.

Chef AJ and Glenn Merzer, *The Secrets to Ultimate Weight Loss*, 2018.

Cromack, George, *Ageing Well*, 2009.

Davis, Brenda, *Defeating Diabetes*, 2003.

Davis, Garth and Howard Jacobson, *Proteinaholic: How Our Obsession with Meat Is Killing Us and What We Can Do About It*, 2015.

Ehret, Arnold, *Mucusless Diet Healing System*, 1976.

Esselstyn, Caldwell B., *Prevent and Reverse Heart Disease*, 2008.

Fuhrman, Joel, *The End of Diabetes*, 2012.

Greger, Michael, *How Not to Die*, 2015.

Greger, Michael, *How Not to Diet*, 2019.

Howell, Edward, *Enzyme Nutrition*, 1985.

Katherine, Anne, *Anatomy of a Food Addiction*, 1991.

Khambatta, Cyrus and Robby Barbaro, *Mastering Diabetes*, 2020.

Lappé, Frances Moore, *Diet for a Small Planet*, 1971.

Lisle, Doug, *The Pleasure Trap*, 2003.

Minich, Deanna, *The Rainbow Diet*, 2017.

Murray-Wakelin, Janette, *Raw Can Cure Cancer*, 2014.

Pierre, John, *The Pillars of Health*, 2013.

Pixie, Magenta, *Lessons from a Living Lemuria*, 2020.

Reinfeld, Mark, *Healing the Vegan Way: Plant-Based Eating for Optimal Health and Wellness*, 2016.

Robbins, John, *Diet for a New America*, 1987.

Wark, Chris, *Chris Beat Cancer*, 2018.

William, Anthony, *Celery Juice*, 2019.

William, Anthony, *Cleanse to Heal*, 2020.

William, Anthony, *Liver Rescue*, 2018.

Documentaries

Eat, Fast, and Live Longer, 2015 Documentary (BBC).

Fat, Sick and Nearly Dead, 2010 Documentary.

Forks Over Knives, 2001 Documentary.

The Game Changers, 2019 Documentary.

Super Size Me, 2004 Documentary.

Websites (as of 2020)

Foodnsport.com/

www.forksoverknives.com

www.NutritionFacts.org (for research on nutrition)

TrueNorth Health Center, www.healthpromoting.com

www.vegparadise.com

Raw Foods

Books

Cousens, Gabriel, *Rainbow Green Live-food Cuisine*, 2003.

Murray-Wakelin, Janette, *Raw Can Cure Cancer: 100% Raw Courage*, 2014.

Perlot, Andrew, *Raw Food Weight Loss & Vitality*, 2012.

Wigmore, Ann, *The Sprouting Book*, 1986.

Websites (as of 2020)

Dr. Douglas N. Graham, https://foodnsport.com/index.php

Kohler, John, www.okraw.com

Tanny, tannyraw.com

Spiritual Eating

Books

Buhner, Steven Harrod, *The Transformational Power of Fasting*, 2012.

Cousens, Gabriel, *Conscious Eating*, 1992.

Cousens, Gabriel, *Spiritual Nutrition*, 2005.

Ewing, Jim PathFinder, *Conscious Food: Sustainable Growing, Spiritual Eating*, 2012.

Jasmuheen, *The Food of Gods*, 2010.

Lad, Usha and Vasant Lad, *Ayurvedic Cooking for Self-Healing*, 2nd ed., 2009.

Maor, Ray, *A Year Without Food*, 2015.

Morris, Madeleine C., *Miracle of Mana-Force: Secret of Wealth, Love and Power*, 1975.

Pixie, Magenta, *Lessons from a Living Lemuria*, 2020.

Reid, Daniel P., *Tao of Health, Sex and Longevity*, 1989.

Tuttle, Will, *The World Peace Diet*, 2005.

Virtue, Doreen and Becky Black, *Eating in the Light*, 2013.

Virtue, Doreen and Robert Reeves, *Nutrition for Intuition*, 2016.

William, Anthony, *Life-Changing Foods*, 2016.

William, Anthony, *Medical Medium*, 2015.

Documentary

Straubinger, PA, *In the Beginning, There was Light*, 2010 (on Vimeo).

The New Earth

Books and Article

Adams, Mark, *Meet Me in Atlantis*, 2015.

Ashalyn & Adama the Telosian, *Adama Discourses*, 2015.

Cannon, Dolores, *The Three Waves of Volunteers and the New Earth*, 2011.

Carwin, James, *Pleiadian Prophecy 2020*, 2016.

Cervé, Wishar S. and James D. Ward, *Lemuria: The Lost Continent of the Pacific*, 1931.

Dodson, Frederick, *Parallel Universes of Self*, 2016.

"The Essenes", *Rosicrucian Digest*, Volume 85, No. 2, 2007.

Frissell, Bob, *Nothing in This Book Is True, But It's Exactly How Things Are*, 2002.

Garber, Michael James, *The Illumination Codex: Guidance for Ascension to New Earth*, 2021.

Heartsong, Claire, *Anna, Grandmother of Jesus*, 2017.

Heartsong, Claire, *Anna, the Voice of the Magdalenes*, 2017.

Jasmuheen, *Pranic Nourishment*, 2012.

Jones, Aurelia Louise, *Telos, Volumes 1 Through 3*, 2004-2006.

Joseph, Frank, *Survivors of Atlantis*, 2004.

Marquez, Eva, *A Starseed Guide, Volume 1*, 2016.

Meurois-Givaudan, Anne and Daniel, *The Way of the Essenes*, 1993.

Milanovich, Norma, Betty Rice and Cynthia Ploski, *We, the Arcturians*, 1990.

Miller, David K., *Connecting with the Arcturians*, 2015.

Mycal Enlightened, *Essentiality I*, 2019.

Pixie, Magenta, *The Black Box Programme and the Rose Gold Flame as Antidote*, 2019.

Pixie, Magenta, *The Infinite Helix and the Emerald Flame*, 2018.

Pixie, Magenta, *Masters of the Matrix*, 2016.

Russell, Walter, *The Universal One*, 1910.

St. Germain, Maureen J., *Waking up in 5D*, 2017.

Scott, Brian, *The Reality Revolution*, 2020.

Szekely, Edmond Bordeaux, ed., *The Essene Gospel of Peace, Books One Through Four*, 1937 to 1981.

Ward, James Douglas and WS Cervé, *Lemuria: The Lost Continent of the Pacific*, 1931.

Wilson, Stuart and Joanna Prentis, *The Essenes: Children of the Light*, 2005.

Biography

Dr. Mike Radice is a licensed minister, Reiki Master Teacher, and Jyorei certified healer. He has a PhD in Public History and Nonprofit Management from The Union Institute & University, a PGC in Museum Studies from New York University, an MS and MA in Mental Health Counseling and School Psychology from Wright State University and a BS in Secondary Education from Miami University (OH). He's written over 30 articles and short stories on psychology, child development and energy healing practices. A native of Greater Cleveland, he now lives in Los Angeles practicing "nonprofit medicine" as a consultant and interim administrator. He also has a private Reiki practice.

O-BOOKS

SPIRITUALITY

O is a symbol of the world, of oneness and unity; this eye represents knowledge and insight. We publish titles on general spirituality and living a spiritual life. We aim to inform and help you on your own journey in this life. If you have enjoyed this book, why not tell other readers by posting a review on your preferred book site?

Recent bestsellers from O-Books are:

Heart of Tantric Sex
Diana Richardson
Revealing Eastern secrets of deep love and intimacy to Western couples.
Paperback: 978-1-90381-637-0 ebook: 978-1-84694-637-0

Crystal Prescriptions
The A-Z guide to over 1,200 symptoms and their healing crystals
Judy Hall
The first in the popular series of eight books, this handy little guide is packed as tight as a pill bottle with crystal remedies for ailments.
Paperback: 978-1-90504-740-6 ebook: 978-1-84694-629-5

Shine On
David Ditchfield and J S Jones
What if the aftereffects of a near-death experience were undeniable? What if a person could suddenly produce high-quality paintings of the afterlife, or if they acquired the ability to compose classical symphonies? Meet: David Ditchfield.
Paperback: 978-1-78904-365-5 ebook: 978-1-78904-366-2

The Way of Reiki
The Inner Teachings of Mikao Usui Frans Stiene
The roadmap for deepening your understanding of the system of Reiki and rediscovering your True Self.
Paperback: 978-1-78535-665-0 ebook: 978-1-78535-744-2

You Are Not Your Thoughts.
Frances Trussell
The journey to a mindful way of being, for those who want to truly know the power of mindfulness.
Paperback: 978-1-78535-816-6 ebook: 978-1-78535-817-3

The Mysteries of the Twelfth Astrological House
Fallen Angels
Carmen Turner-Schott, MSW, LISW
Everyone wants to know more about the most misunderstood house in astrology — the twelfth astrological house.
Paperback: 978-1-78099-343-0 ebook: 978-1-78099-344-7

WhatsApps from Heaven
Louise Hamlin
An account of a bereavement and the extraordinary signs —
including WhatsApps — that a retired law lecturer received from
her deceased husband.
Paperback: 978-1-78904-947-3 ebook: 978-1-78904-948-0

The Holistic Guide to Your Health & Wellbeing Today
Oliver Rolfe
A holistic guide to improving your complete health, both inside
and out.
Paperback: 978-1-78535-392-5 ebook: 978-1-78535-393-2

Cool Sex
Diana Richardson and Wendy Doeleman
For deeply satisfying sex, the real secret is to reduce the heat, to
cool down. Discover the empowerment and fulfilment of sex with
loving mindfulness.
Paperback: 978-1-78904-351-8 ebook: 978-1-78904-352-5

Creating Real Happiness A to Z
Stephani Grace
Creating Real Happiness A to Z will help you understand the
truth that you are not your ego (conditioned self).
Paperback: 978-1-78904-951-0 ebook: 978-1-78904-952-7

A Colourful Dose of Optimism
Jules Standish
It's time for us to look on the bright side, by boosting our mood
and lifting our spirit, both in our interiors, as well as in our closet.
Paperback: 978-1-78904-927-5 ebook: 978-1-78904-928-2

Readers of ebooks can buy or view any of these bestsellers by
clicking on the live link in the title. Most titles are published in
paperback and as an ebook. Paperbacks are available in
traditional bookshops. Both print and ebook formats are available
online.

Find more titles and sign up to our readers' newsletter at
www.o-books.com

Follow O books on Facebook at **O-books**

For video content, author interviews and more, please subscribe to our YouTube channel:

O-BOOKS Presents

Follow us on social media for book news, promotions and more:

Facebook: O-Books

Instagram: @o_books_mbs

Twitter: @obooks

Tik Tok: @ObooksMBS

www.o-books.com